Dawn Nashnay

254

Made in Thailand

On the map Thailand looks like an unfolding lotus, growing up into Asia from its stem on the Malay Peninsula. In reality, Thailand — once known as Siam — is a rough, dense, tropical land of great forests, alluvial plains, twisting rivers, and wooded mountains. But from the people who live on those rich plains and musky, damp swamplands have come some of the East's most exquisite silks, colorful paintings, intricate architecture, silver and gold jewelry, teakwood carvings, and strong stone sculptures.

The land and the neighboring countries have contributed to the hardiness of the Thai and their culture, a culture that has survived wars, enslavements, and the subtle influences of three religions — spirit worship, Brahmanism, and Buddhism.

Margaret Ayer has skillfully woven the colorful threads of Thai history, religion, and geography into a rich tapestry forming the country's arts and crafts.

Other books in this series are:

MADE IN CANADA by Mary Graham Bonner
MADE IN CHINA by Cornelia Spencer
MADE IN ICELAND by Grace Golden
MADE IN INDIA by Cornelia Spencer
MADE IN ITALY by Frances Toor
MADE IN JAPAN by Cornelia Spencer
MADE IN MEXICO by Patricia Fent Ross

Made in Thailand

written and illustrated by Margaret Ayer

and with photographs

Alfred A. Knopf, New York

To my best friend in Thailand,
H.H. Princess Pilai Diskul.

13

Grateful acknowledgment is made for permission to use the following photographs:

The Asia Society Performing Arts Program, 139, 142
Ira Ayer, 66
Black Star: Ifor, 216; Hal Linker, 169; Marie Mattson, frontis., 48, 59, 211;
  Barry Schuttler, 173; Ace Williams, 92
Metropolitan Museum of Art, 76, 82, 115, 117, 224, 226
Monkmeyer Press Photo Service: Ted Bank, 33; Fujihira, 68, 72; Wendy Hilty, 5;
  Marie Wilson, 145
Tourist Organization of Thailand, Bangkok, 26, 57, 96, 130
United Nations, 37, 61, 78, 162, 164, 189, 205, 212, 236

Library of Congress Catalog Card Number: 62-9470

THIS IS A BORZOI BOOK, PUBLISHED BY ALFRED A. KNOPF, INC.

Acknowledgments

I would like to express my grateful appreciation to the people who have helped me in the research for this book:

Prince Subhadradis Diskul, Director of the Thai National Art Museum, took time to answer many questions for me. And Princess Pilai Diskul, guiding and interpreting for me, enabled me to find many things I could not have seen without her aid.

Princess Poon Diskul, who was the head of the Buddhist Society of Thailand, very kindly read and checked my chapter on Buddhism, and translated the legend of *The Jealous Rice-bird*, found in chapter eleven, for me.

Mr. David Morton of the Institute of Ethnomusicology of the University of California, and an expert on Thai music, read and helped me with the chapter on music.

Mr. Dhanit Yupho, Director General of Fine Arts, enabled me to visit the Art School and classes in Thai dancing, and to see the dancers dress in their costumes and prepare for a performance. He also gave me a series of booklets on Thai arts. I would also like to thank Mr. Sanum Sumitr, Director General of Vocational Education, who showed me students at work on Thai crafts.

Mr. J. J. Boeles of the Siam Society Research Center, helped me to find material and information in the Society library.

Mr. Jim Thompson of the Thai Silk Company, gave me valuable information about the silk-weaving industry, and Mr. Kurt Neuenschwander of the same company, took me with him on his tour of inspection to the village of the silk workers and explained the various processes of weaving and dyeing.

Acknowledgments

Thai Nakon, Court Jewelers, showed me around their workshop, and the S. Samron Bronze Company, makers of bronze products, took me around their factory.

Miss Amara of the Tourist Organization, helped me in the selection of photographs which the Department kindly donated for this book.

My husband, Alfred Babington Smith, who once worked for a teak-exporting company in Thailand, gave me valuable information and also helped me with the typing of the manuscript.

I wish to thank the many others whose names I never knew, who aided me so pleasantly while I was in Thailand on my recent visit to the country, and also the many friends who helped me to understand and love Thailand when it was my home years ago.

And last, I would like to mention my mother and my father, Dr. Ira Ayer, with grateful and affectionate memory, who introduced me to Thailand.

Contents

Made in Thailand

1

Thailand, the Country of the Free

"It takes many ingredients to make a fine dish of curry."

The name of Thailand, or *Muang Thai* as it is called in the language of the country, means the "Land of the Free." Unlike most of Southeast Asia, it has never been the colony of a Western nation. Before the name was changed in 1939, it was known as Siam.

On the map it looks like an unfolding lotus, growing up into Asia from its stem on the Malay Peninsula. It has a population of twenty-three million people and an area of about two hundred thousand square miles.

Bangkok, the capital city, is on the main river of Thailand, about twenty miles from the Gulf of Siam. It has one-and-a-half million inhabitants and is one of the major air centers of the Orient. Chiengmai, in the north, is the next largest city and was once, long ago, the capital of an independent principality. Except for these two large cities, there are only thirty towns in Thailand with a population of over ten thousand. They are situated mostly on the coast or along rivers in the central part of Thailand.

Central Thailand is a large alluvial plain, once forested, but now riceland, drained by many rivers and canals. It is the chief commercial rice-growing region of the country.

During the wet season in the summer, flooding water brings fertilizing silt to the land.

The rice areas are divided into fields by low banks called *bunds*. In hilly country, fields are terraced to make them flat. In the plains, the land stretches endlessly to the horizon, broken by clumps of bamboo, palms, and trees, and by occasional farmhouses and temples. These houses and temples are raised a few feet above the surface of the plain by earth taken from the canals. Farmers stand knee-deep in the brown water, covered with mud, working to keep the channels from silting up, and removing water plants that choke the waterways.

All life seems to depend on the rich, fecund mud, and to have evolved from it. Even houses have weathered to its color. Buffaloes lie in muddy wallows when they are not working. In the dry season, when the earth is packed hard, the muddy waterways keep life going.

The immense sky dominates the landscape, and the great distances make people and buffaloes look like toys from a Noah's Ark.

Plateaus rise around the plain. On these, agriculture is more varied and livestock is raised. Beyond, there are hills and rugged mountains covered with forests.

The great forests which cover nearly three-quarters of Thailand are of original growth. They protect the land from erosion and furnish many products for home use and commerce. The characteristic types of forests merge into each other. In the south and on the peninsula the rain forests grow, always green from the abundance of rainfall. Great, straight tree trunks rise almost branchless up to

*A farmer in his rice fields stands knee-deep in the
muddy water, removing plants that choke the waterway.*

their spreading crowns. Below, in the dense shade, smaller trees fight for life, struggle for more sunlight. Vines twist about and ferns cling to the tree trunks.

Along the coasts and low banks of the rivers the rank growth is almost impenetrable and forms thick walls of tangled green. Tall trees push above the green brush, many flowering in masses of red, yellow, or pink.

Further north, in the highlands and mountains, the monsoon winds bring alternate seasons of dry and wet weather. Here the monsoon forests grow. The trees are mostly deciduous, with dense undergrowth. At first, when the wet season begins, the rain comes gradually, then becomes a continuous downpour that lasts for days. Everything is drenched by the walls of water, the tracks turn into small torrents, and the streams are impassable. When the sun comes out, mist rises like steam from the valleys. The sopping land hardly dries out before the pounding rain slaps down again. Nomadic jungle tribes scatter through the forests, clearing a few fields for crops or building small settlements.

The few trails through the forest are frightening, for one can only see a short distance ahead. The forests are frequented by wild animals. The tribesmen are convinced that the forests are also full of mischievous or evil nature-spirits. Who knows what unseen creature may cause the sudden crack of a twig? In the deep gulches, the streams slipping over the rocks sound like many voices talking together, though no one is there. The tribesmen wear amulets for protection from dangers real and unreal.

The very real danger is from wild animals. Rhinoceroses lurk in the forests, away from man. Many kinds of monkeys swing through the trees, babies clinging to their mothers. They flee with angry cries when they suddenly catch sight of a tiger, its yellow and black stripes hardly visible in the undergrowth's streaks of light. Or they will see a still more ferocious panther. In the remote mountains fierce wild buffaloes roam, looking very much like the tame ones that small boys drive across the rice fields. Elephants crash through the countryside, afraid of no other animal.

There are many varieties of deer. The tiny, shy mouse deer, not truly a deer at all, is only a little over a foot high. It has no antlers, but the male has tiny tusks. Its little sides are dappled like a fawn's, and it sneaks about in fear of many enemies.

There are big hornbills in the forest; and parakeets, streaks of color, dart about. Weaverbirds' nests hang like old brown socks from the branches.

Boas tangle with the creepers; cobras and smaller snakes slip through the growth on the ground. The Thai think that all snakes are dangerous and avoid them, although only one species in seven is harmful; but this seems quite enough to worry a person!

The air is full of the hum and throb of unseen insects. Butterflies flit about like blossoms falling from the tall trees, and bumbling moths come out at night.

The forested mountains form part of the northwest boundary between Thailand and its neighbors. Thailand's boundaries have shifted back and forth during many wars fought with the surrounding countries: Burma, Laos, Cambodia, and Malaya.

The early history of Thailand is vague. The Thai, an agricultural race, originated in China. Over hundreds of years they gradually migrated southward to escape the domination of the Chinese and to seek fertile land. They spread

over much of southeast Asia early in the twelfth century.
Scattering about through central Thailand, they estab-
lished towns under chieftains. Their religion was a mixture of spirit worship and Buddhism.

The area in which the Thai settled was an outpost of
the great Khmer Empire that stretched through much of
the land that today has become Thailand and Cambodia.

The origin of the Khmer Empire is not known. It was
first an agricultural country, but when the Thai came in
contact with them, the Khmers had become highly cul-
tured. Khmer learning, art, and religion, both Buddhist
and Brahman, had come from India, brought by traders
who had followed ancient routes and had carried on commerce with Cambodia for centuries. The traders had settled in the country to raise families there, intermarrying
with the Khmers.

The Thai became vassals of the Khmers for several hundred years, and were forced to give tribute and to supply
labor to help in the erection of the enormous buildings of
the Khmers. The remains of these carved stone temples
and cities still stand in Thailand and Cambodia, monuments to Khmer skill in architecture and sculpture.

During this time the Thai learned many arts and techniques from the superior civilization of the Khmers, and
the Brahman religion merged with the Thai beliefs in
Buddhism and animism.

In the thirteenth century some of the Thai chieftains
banded together, rebelled against the Khmers, and founded
the first Thai nation, whose center was the city of Sukhodaya. Phra Ruang became king in 1276. Many legends
grew up about him, and he is a popular hero in Thailand
today. The kingdom prospered and grew powerful during
his leadership. An inscribed stone carved during his reign

has been found. It describes Sukhodaya as a land of plenty: "the waters full of fish; the fields yield rice; the King takes no advantage of the people, and they are bright with happiness."

A great gong hung before the gate of the palace, and any subject who had a plea to lay before the king could strike it. The king would give the supplicant an audience and a personal judgment in any matter.

The kingdom of Sukhodaya spread out, influenced by trading contacts with Burma, China, and India. After about one hundred years, the power of the city-state declined. In 1378, after one hundred and forty years of independence, it became Ayudhya's vassal. The kingdom of Ayudhya had been founded in 1340 by the ruler of the city, Rama Tibodi, who had himself proclaimed king. He soon was so strong that he ruled much of the country that is Thailand today.

The boundaries of the city-states, governed by princes, were not definite. The city-states were far from Ayudhya and under its loose authority. They owed tribute to its king and provided forced labor when demanded. The northern principalities were sometimes independent, sometimes vassals of Ayudhya or Burma. This was rather similar to the feudal system in Europe.

To retain his powers, the king of Ayudhya had to have command of the spreading river system of the plains, the chief route of communication.

The northern cities of the country were important to both Ayudhya and Burma. The Burmese attempted to hold them for heavy supplies could not be brought through the rough mountain passes on the border. It was necessary for these cities to furnish supplies which were then carried by boat along the rivers, following the armies that marched southward toward Ayudhya. Both armies destroyed anything along the way that might be of use to the enemy, in a scorched-earth policy. The border lands were so often ravaged and laid waste that today the area is still without towns. Today the wind sighs through tall, coarse grass and scrub forests that are said to be full of the ghosts of the hordes that died there.

Whenever Ayudhya was involved in a war with Burma, the Khmers took the opportunity to harass and raid the eastern provinces. Ayudhya finally conquered Cambodia in 1593, destroyed the capital city of Angkor Thom, carried away riches, made the country a vassal state, and brought back ninety thousand captives and artisans.

The policy of warfare at that time was to sack cities, destroying the protective walls by using strong elephants to batter down the gate. Many thousands of the population were taken prisoner and resettled in the victor's country. In this way, ideas and techniques of arts and crafts were exchanged; the culture of one state influenced the other. The kings of Ayudhya borrowed the pomp and ceremonies of the Brahman Khmers. They also borrowed the idea that the monarchy was semidivine, a very different concept than the paternalism of their early kings.

Ayudhya was a fortified city encircled by massive walls with watchtowers and forts and surrounded by river and canals — an island city. It had a million inhabitants and survived many attacks. It seemed impregnable. It had been the strongest city in the country for over four hundred years under thirty-three kings. A large and prosperous place, it was enriched with hundreds of gorgeous temples, spires, and palaces. Beautiful works of art had accumulated there; endless riches in the king's treasury; books on law, religion, history, and literature in the library.

After half a century of peace, a great Burmese army fought its way to the city and besieged it. Ayudhya held out for two years. In 1767, with the people and garrison starving and weakened by epidemics, the city could no longer resist. The Burmese entered the city, sacking it, looting, setting raging fires. The king was killed and the streets were filled with dead people. Only a fraction of the inhabitants were left. When the city was in ruins, the Burmese left for home, leaving a few scattered garrisons.

They carried away all the city's portable riches, including a vast number of captives. The art of centuries had been destroyed: the library of priceless books burned; mural paintings vanished in flames; temples and palaces torn apart for the gold adornments. It seemed as though the Thai nation would never recover from this disaster.

Ayudhya was never rebuilt as a city. Today there is a village strung out along the river and canals that formerly protected the city. Some roads run inland. There are a few modern government buildings. Everywhere the ancient haunts the new. Old parts of walls stand, defending nothing since that long-ago defeat. Salvaged statues of Buddha, their rich temples long gone, sit indifferently beneath simple wooden roofs.

There are many square miles of ruins where the jungle, inhabited by birds and lizards that flick over the hot stones, tries to creep back. Gates stand, leading to a few columns that once supported the splendid roofs of palaces and temples. Nearby there is a small wooden shrine which was recently erected to the spirit of the land.

Solid towers called *Phra Prangs*, which contained relics, still stand. Some have been cleared of the vines that tangled about them, and of their crowns of bushes. They are no longer covered with gold and magnificent decorations, but the long-shaped rosy bricks of the foundations appear through gray stucco.

The largest sitting Buddha in the world, once covered with eight hundred pounds of gold, until lately sat on a ruined pedestal under the open sky. The figure is now inside a newly-constructed temple to which worshipers flock. Its eyes look high above the heads of the crowd. The figure seems indifferent whether homage is offered today by free Thai clad in cotton or by kings and nobles in rich garments.

After the fall of Ayudhya, most of the Burmese army withdrew to Burma. The Burmese had become involved in a war against invading Chinese. This helped the Thai in their campaigns against Burmese-held garrisons in Thailand. The Thai crown was offered by the leaders of the Thai army to one of its most capable generals, Phra Taksin, who became king. He chose a site for the new capital fifty miles down the river from the old ruined capital. Bangkok stands there today. A brave and competent man, Phra Taksin unfortunately became suspicious and cruel even to members of his own family, and finally mad. He spent long hours in prayer, hoping to enable himself to fly through the sky. There was a revolt. Phra Taksin was deposed in 1782 and executed. His body was cremated with royal honors.

Another great leader then became king. General Chakri, who called himself Rama I, founded the present dynasty of Thailand.

King Rama I planned to make Bangkok a fine city, as much like the lost Ayudhya as possible. The river swept in a great loop around the site of the city. A canal connecting the ends of the loop was cut across, making Bangkok an island city. The new capital was fortified with walls and was further protected by surrounding swampland. The palace and temples were built in the old architectural tradition by the best artists and craftsmen available, and adorned with carving, murals, and molded decorations. It took many years to erect Bangkok's fine buildings, but they still stand today.

Salvaging everything possible from the fallen Ayudhya, King Rama I restored the arts, laws, and canons of religion. He set up a commission to work out the complicated Brahman rites connected with royalty. The nation rose again from the ashes of its former glory.

Before the king's coronation, even the traditional objects of the royal regalia had to be made to replace those carried away by the Burmese. The regalia contains many jewel-encrusted gold crowns, a "Sword of Victory" which hangs from a jeweled belt, and various weapons — a spear, a bow, a trident (the symbol of the god Siva), and a sharp-edged discus.

Even slippers are part of the symbolic regalia, for shoes at one time were not worn by the common people, and

only the king could wear shoes in the palace. There are also fans and emblematic flywhisks, made of a yak's tail and the tail of a dead white elephant. (Both the yak and the white elephant are considered propitious animals.) For the king's personal use there are betel sets, a vessel to hold sacred water, and an urn, all made of gold or silver. Finally, there is a flat gold sheet inscribed with the king's name and his scores of long, august, and flattering titles.

One result of the warfare was the spreading of art forms. Artists and craftsmen were part of the booty brought back from campaigns. They were resettled in the conqueror's country and either given land or made slaves.

A freeman was required to give his time, instead of taxes, to the king — usually a few months a year. A craftsman could donate this time to an overlord or to the temple. Often the lord was his patron. This system gave an artisan a chance to do slow, careful work, as all his needs were cared for. It did not matter how long he took to finish a task.

Although Thailand has always been chiefly an agricultural country, a list dating from the time of Ayudhya names the many trades and crafts that were carried on. There were wood carvers, silversmiths, goldsmiths and coppersmiths, workers in precious stones and lacquer, fresco painters and decorators, weavers, dyers, perfumers, tanners, potters, carpenters, boatbuilders, and ropemakers. There were musicians, dancers, actors, astrologers, magicians, and elephant trainers. There were workers in sugar factories, limekilns, iron foundries, and brickyards. Most of these trades are carried on today.

Art was a cultural rather than an individual expression. Traditional forms were carried on from one generation to another, subjects repeated over and over again. But even these could differ, indicating the individuality of the maker. Gradual changes took place during the centuries, and the names of Sukhodaya, Ayudhya, and Bangkok have been given to styles and periods of art.

Artists were anonymous before the nineteenth century. The Buddhist religion did not encourage individualism — the work was the important thing. This transitory life was of no importance; a man's personality was forgotten after his death. An artist was supposed to be devoted to his craft, and religious works were considered an act of merit and devotion, both for the artist and the patron. Erecting a temple was thought to be an extremely meritorious act, both for the sponsor and the men who worked upon it. The temple grounds and buildings were adorned with the greatest works of the period in which they were built.

Members of the nobility were the chief patrons of the arts — especially the king — and the art reflected the tastes of the upper classes. Artists and artisans of all kinds were attached to the court. They made jewelry and beautiful, elaborate objects for ceremonial or personal use.

Religious thought has had a great influence on all the arts. Buddhism has been the strongest element in Thai religion, but its symbols and legends merge with those of Brahmanism. These all intermingle in the arts of Thailand.

Although the Thai artist was influenced by the ideas of surrounding countries and his religion, he had a natural creative ability. Distinct Thai art forms developed, rich and vigorous.

The artist observed nature, and in observing the animals of the country, he gave reality and strength to the oft-portrayed mythological animals. The lushness of the tropical vegetation is reflected in conventional foliage, inter-

laced in patterns full of rhythm. Abstract designs have
well-balanced lines and spaces. One popular motif looks
like a flickering flame, or many flames, flowing upwards,
and is called *kranok*. The leaves, blossoms, and pods of
the lotus, associated with Buddhism, are an inspiration for
many designs and architectural ornaments.

During the best periods of Thai art, the love of decoration was subordinated to form and function, but later, in
the eighteenth century, when art started to decline, over-
elaborate decoration was used for its own sake, a tendency
in all decadent art.

Anything made well to fulfill its function usually
achieves beauty also. The many simple things made and
used by the Thai peasant-artisan have this beauty.

2

The Thai

"You cannot see gold tied in a cloth, and the best of man is often beneath his skin."

The Thai are friendly and have gracious, dignified manners. When they meet, they raise their hands in greeting, palms together toward the face, and bend forward in a bow. They are gay, with a sense of humor, and always ready for a good time. The Thai admire quick-wittedness, self-reliance, modesty, and moderation in living. They like a "cool heart" that avoids aggression, anger, and hatred. Generosity, they feel, should be practiced cheerfully and willingly. Any regrets take away from the merit of the action. Children are taught good manners early, but are not trained with severity.

Old people are proud of advanced age. The elderly are treated with respect and admired by younger people, who fetch and carry for them; the youngsters take over many of the tasks their elders used to do. In return, grandparents care for the small children when the mother works.

In appearance the Thai are slight and graceful with pale tan skins, brown eyes, and straight, black hair. Men and boys wear their hair short. Small girls have bobbed hair, as do many of the younger women; an older woman may have long hair twisted into a knot in back. Permanent waves are very popular, and most teen-age girls yearn for one. No one wears a hat except for working in the sun, in which case the women wear large straw hats, like flat-topped baskets. They wish to be protected from the sun and not become too brown, for fair skin in Thailand is a sign of beauty.

Some of the countrypeople go barefooted, but most of the Thai wear Japanese sandals. Some of the women wear fancy Western-style sandals. The men and boys wear sandals or sneakers, and sometimes Western shoes. They wear shorts or trousers made of white duck, khaki, or dark cloth, and a shirt or singlet either tucked inside the trousers or hanging outside. In the larger towns, clothing is becoming steadily Westernized.

In the northern part of the country, women have always worn a sarong-like skirt called a *pasin* folded about them. Most modern Thai girls and women have adopted this garment and wear it with a blouse. With her best clothes the Thai woman wears a silver belt and as much jewelry as she can afford.

Many women and girls have taken to wearing blouses and skirts or dresses. Throughout the country, most women own at least one dress as well as the traditional garments. Thai garments all look fresh and starched, as if they had just come from the laundry. Although many of the Thai wear modern clothes in the office or at social gatherings, they revert to the comfortable native clothes at home.

A *panung*, which used to be worn by both men and women in Thailand, and is still seen in rural districts, is considered as old-fashioned as a sunbonnet is to us. It is made of a strip of cloth a yard wide and two yards long, and is folded about the lower part of the body. The edge hangs below the knees, and at the front of the waist two nips of cloth are twisted together. Then the ends are wound together, brought between the legs, and tucked into the waistline in back. The effect is something like a very long and loose loincloth. Peasant women often wear the panung in the fields, with a long-sleeved, dark blouse.

Peasant men have a strip of cloth, plaid or striped, which is used in many ways — as a belt, as a turban to keep sweat from running into their eyes during hot work, or as a loincloth when fishing or bathing. A baby wears little or nothing until he is a year or two old — maybe a little shirt, a charm around his neck, and an anklet.

Primary education is compulsory for Thai children when they reach eight years of age. The smallest girls usually wear a dark blue jumper-dress over a white blouse to school; the older ones, a blue skirt and a middy. The boys usually wear dark blue shorts and a white shirt. They hurry to school cheerfully, carrying briefcases or airplane bags.

Before the villages had schools for both boys and girls, with teachers trained at the Government College of Education, the monks taught the boys at the temples. It was a regular part of their work. The girls learned what they could at home. Now monks only teach religious subjects.

Each town must furnish its own school building. Because of this, a number of the smaller villages hold school in one of the buildings in the temple enclosure.

Many of the same subjects are taught in Thailand as in the United States. Crafts used to be learned at home, but now these are taught at the schools, too. Children can learn basketry, mat weaving, carpentry, and how to make household articles.

The majority of children leave school when they have completed the four years of primary education. In order

to enter the secondary schools, they must pass an examination set by the government. They all learn English at
these secondary schools.

The brightest children can go on to one of a number of
universities or vocational colleges. They may take courses
in law, medicine, science, commerce, or public administration. There is an Arts and Crafts School, a Technical Institute (which is considered the best in Southeast Asia),
and an Agricultural College that also teaches forestry and
fishery.

Today women as well as men have the vote in Thailand.
Thai women have always been free and independent,
except for the women of the ancient nobility, who were
subject to many restrictions.

Polygamy is fast dying out. The majority of Thai have
always been monogamous in practice; only the wealthy
could afford many wives and families. Although young
people select their own mates, they usually do not go
against the wishes of their parents. Marriage is a civil
contract, but frequently the monks are asked to give a
blessing with ceremonies and feasting.

Middle-class women now hold positions as teachers,
nurses, clerical workers in offices, and salesgirls in shops.
They have always worked at weaving, pottery, and other
crafts, as well as helping with farming. Household crafts
occupy the farmer and his family between the busiest
seasons of farmwork. They take the goods that they do not
need to the local market.

The market may be a permanent structure, open at the
sides and covered by a thatched roof. The merchandise
is sold from wooden platforms which are raised about

eighteen inches above the packed earth floor. Rays of sunlight filter through cracks in the roof, like spotlights, touching the fruits and vegetables with streaks of bright color. In small towns, the market is not under a permanent structure. Instead, it may be held in the village square, where the goods are spread out on mats and boards across trestles that can be removed at the end of the day. Cotton awnings spread across a corner or a large, oiled umbrella furnish shade for the merchant.

The Thai show their natural sense of design even in the arrangement of their wares. In a basket, bunches of bananas, the points upwards, circle to a narrow dome at the top, as decorative as the *repoussé* cover of a Thai silver bowl. Noodles spiral in neat coils, and dark green betel leaves, folded into cones, neatly fill a satiny mound of banana leaves. Fruits and vegetables are piled in rounded heaps. Papayas and pineapples, laced into raffia nets, hang in bunches from poles which support the roof. Canned goods, with Thai or Chinese labels, are piled in checkered columns, more neatly than in any Western supermarket.

A big, flat basket hangs behind a stall with the owner's name and a list of his goods painted on it. In the larger markets, sellers of each type of goods keep together, and each section has a different smell. There is the pleasant scent of fruit, and the starchy smell of piled bolts of cotton goods and the clothing which hangs overhead. Pickles in enamel basins fill the air with acid odors, and pungent spices add their note. The smell of the fish-sellers' wares spreads around their damp stalls. There are green shrimp and pink dried shrimp; putty-colored or pinkish fish pastes piled on trays; all sizes of silvery, shining fish stare with cold, dead eyes from baskets, or are hung in rows on racks. They all accent the acrid, overpowering smell of dried fish.

It is a relief to pass on to an array of baskets and mats, past ironware and pots, and reach the fragrant flower stalls, with their buckets and baskets full of color. There are musky-sweet pink lotus; gardenias, frangipani, and tuberoses full of perfume; and bright African daisies, pink, blue, or red, looking as though they were cut from crisp paper. Girls sit beside the baskets threading small flowers on long steel knitting needles, placing them in spirals, winding them about in different-colored bands. They make bracelets, necklaces, and long, slender wreaths for offerings to the temple. Each floral fantasy is finished with a drooping tassel that ends in a large flower.

But all these real flowers are not enough for the Thai. The deft fingers of the girls make artificial flowers out of parts of real ones. Petals and stamens are arranged into flowers that were never seen growing — copies of the old designs. The flowers are made with such delicacy that the petals are not bruised, and the artificial blossoms look as fresh as any that have been picked in the garden.

Petals of many colors are made into intricate mosaic patterns that are pressed onto damp clay in a silver bowl. Floral cones are made to cover gifts to the temple.

Women stroll along the narrow alleys, carrying baskets, babies astride the hip, children tagging after. They may pause at a stand for a drink of soda pop; the children suck sweets held in bits of banana leaf. The market is not just for buying and selling, it is a sociable meeting place. Murmuring voices exchange gossip. Occasionally a child cries, or a bird twitters in a bamboo cage. A green parrot may squeak; its head — pink, with a dark line where it joins the neck — looks as though it might be unscrewed easily. A cock crows lazily from under a wide domed basket.

Every transaction involves friendly arguments, as much as a game as a business. Soon both buyer and seller are satisfied, though the buyer goes off mumbling that she has spent too much of the family money, and the market-woman grumbles that she has made no profit at all.

Small villages may combine and use one market together, meeting informally on one day of the week. Many rural villages have less than one hundred houses. The farmers like to group their houses together, a preference that may have started when towns were fortified and it was not safe to live beyond their walls. Towns are strung out along a waterway or a road, or are clustered together amid the fields, shaded by palms and fruit trees.

Most farmers own their own land. As Thailand is not overpopulated, as so many Oriental countries are, there is little real poverty. A farmer can supply most of his own simple necessities.

The people in the rural villages keep to traditional ways. There are scanty furnishings in their small houses. There are no closets; the few extra garments and cotton blankets for the cool season are kept in a wooden chest. Hooks or a length of bamboo hold the clothes that are used every day. Extra goods, jars or baskets, and small tools are thrust onto the rafters overhead. Larger things and farm equipment are stored beneath the house. This area is an extra room for the family and a stable for the animals.

The family sits on the polished floor which is made of wood or split bamboo. There may be mats or padded cushions to sit upon. Kitchen equipment is simple.

The Thai are very clean people and bathe each day in a waterway if one is near; they wear yesterday's clothes into the water, changing to fresh ones afterwards. Inside, the bathing corner of a house holds a large clay jar of water, which is emptied with a dipper. The water drips down through the slatted floor to the ground below.

A statue of Buddha stands on a shelf. Before it are placed offerings of incense and flowers. The figure is treated with the utmost respect, but no prayer is said or service held there. One's feet must never point toward the figure, either when one is sitting on the floor or sleeping.

Their mats are either of straw or thin pads, with a mosquito net hung above. They are rolled up and put away in the daytime. The small baby sleeps in a cradle hung from the rafters. The cradle has an oblong wooden base, loose-woven, cotton-mesh sides, and is attached to the rafters with cord. It is cool on hot days, and the mother or sister can give it a swing as she passes by.

A kerosene lamp or lantern furnishes light at night. It attracts thousands of insects that flap and batter about. (Some of the insects fall victim to the lamp's flame, and others are caught by the darting tongues of the lizards that scamper about over the walls and ceilings. These lizards are small, gray *chinchucks*, named for the clicking sounds they make. They hide in the cracks and corners in the daytime.)

Wealthier village families have a few more possessions — a gilded altar for the Buddha, an ornament or two, a pressure lamp instead of a lantern, some chairs and a table, and a raised bedstead. The wife may own a treasured sewing machine and a charcoal iron. There may even be a battery-run radio.

Thai houses are built high above the ground on stilts to keep out stray animals, and they have wide eaves to shade them from the outside glare. There is always a veranda

The Lacquer Pavillion at Suan Pakkad Palace, once a
library building, stands high above the ground on stilts.

where much of the family living takes place. A jar of water
stands at the foot of the ladderlike steps, and everyone
splashes water onto his feet to wash off dust before entering the house. The steps are uneven in number for the
Thai believe that evil spirits only like even numbers. There
must also be an odd number of rooms, doors, and windows. There is no glass in the windows. Shutters or a
hinged flap, attached to the top of the frame, are closed
to keep out wind and rain.

Houses have steep, gabled roofs. A row of jars stands
below to catch rain water. The roofs are covered with

thatch made of attap fronds. The side walls are of woven basketwork or also thatched with attap. This palm grows in marshlands and far inland along rivers, rising straight from the water without any trunk, a wall of green. It is a cheap and efficient building material.

Better houses may have tile roofs and walls of paneled teak, the gable ends finished with a strip of wood, curving up to points at the ends. Each room is built on one side of an open space which is part of the floor of the building. Each side has a separate roof. It looks like three houses joined together.

It is pleasant to live in a house by a waterway. Half the house overhangs the water which laps at the landing steps and gently bumps the *sampan* against the posts. Foliage crowds to the water's edge. The family is in and out of the water all day. From the lowest steps of the landing the housewife can wash the dishes, vegetables, or the laundry while she enjoys the traffic on the flowing thoroughfare. She can call out greetings to the people passing by in boats or question them about their business and destination. If she does not wish to go to market, she can buy what she needs from peddlers who bring their boats to her door. Or she may paddle the sampan to the open-fronted shops of the long, narrow village, bargaining for merchandise without leaving her boat.

In the crowded center of the village, the houses huddle together. There is a jumble of gabled roofs running in every direction, with ells and lean-tos built to suit the available land and the owners' whim. Narrow boardwalks run from building to building and across narrow inlets, winding back through land thick with foliage and flowering trees. Ladders lead up to piers that jut out into the water. Some of the piers are covered with peaked roofs. Bridges span the water, high enough to allow a roofed cargo boat to pass underneath. A bridge may consist of a single plank resting on crosspieces held by stakes. A plank at each end reaches down to the low banks.

A bridge may lead to a temple, old and crumbling with the dignity of age or recently repaired and bright with whitewash and gilt surfaces. People sit about gossiping and enjoying the temple grounds or even working. A group of women may sit folding banana leaves in bales to sell for use as wrappings for parcels or as food containers.

In some of the river towns there are floating houses built on pontoons, handsome and expensive structures. They are made of teak, paneled and varnished a shiny brown, with two parallel roofs joined together at the eaves. The roof in front extends over a decklike platform. Doors across the front, sliding in grooves, can be pushed back, opening the front to the river. These floating houses are mainly shops.

Bangkok in the middle of the last century was chiefly a city of waterways. At one time there were eighty thousand floating dwellings on the main canals and lined up three-deep along the banks of the river. Each rested on a thick raft made of several layers of bamboo, to keep the house above the splashings of the water. Several rafts were tied together and attached to piles driven into the mud. The houses rose and fell with the tides that came up the river from the sea. The front row was mostly shops with goods openly displayed to tempt buyers. Only a few shabby houses are left, now, erected on the shore. It is hard to tell that they ever floated on the water.

Life in Bangkok and the large towns is changing rapidly, and the urban Thai are adopting Western ways. Many have substantial houses of brick or stucco, with electricity, running water, refrigeration, and sometimes even air conditioning. They have chairs, tables, beds, and other Western furnishings. High walls and gardens shut them away from the noisy roads outside, or the house and grounds may be behind a row of shops and entered into through a gateway. The furnishings are a mixture of Thailand and the West. The customs of living today swing back and forth between the two cultures.

3

The Thai Eat

"Rice from the land, fish from the water."

Rice is the staple food of Thailand. There is plenty to feed the country and enough is left to export — nearly a million tons a year.

Planting begins at the start of the rainy season, when great massive clouds pile up in the sky. They tower like gleaming mountains where the gods dwell. The sky seems more solid than the ground; the ground vaguely reflects the clouds as more and more fields are flooded and shimmer under rising heat waves. Then, in the evening, the air is full of the croaking of thousands of frogs, little fluting ones and great booming ones, a raucous orchestra of sound.

The farmer thinks it most important to please or propitiate the spirits that may influence the harvests. Ceremonies to insure good crops are among the most ancient of rites, used in some form all over the world since man first planted his food. Many old superstitions still remain in rural Thailand. The farmer says that the rice has a spirit and the seed is its child. He makes offerings to the spirit of the land before he breaks the earth with his plow; he places a cone of banana leaves holding food, flowers, and tobacco in a corner of the nursery field. Small bamboo flags on staffs are stuck among the ripening grains to ward off evil, and the farmer erects a figure of straw and bamboo on the threshing floor, bringing it offerings of the best grains of rice.

Once, elaborate plowing ceremonies were held each year in the capital. Although no longer considered essential, they are occasionally held for the sake of tradition. Like so many Thai ceremonies, this one was brought from India centuries ago.

At first the ceremony was conducted in Thailand by the king himself. Then he named a high court official to take his place. For three days the official ruled as temporary king, with all the privileges of royalty, while the real king remained in his palace. The temporary king owned the cargoes of any ship arriving in the harbor during that period, and he could take anything he wanted from a shop that was open, so one can be sure that most of the shops were tightly shuttered.

Today the Minister of Agriculture plows the first furrows that start the rice season.

After the ceremony the government gives any farmer who wishes it bags of superior rice seed to improve the quality of the harvest.

Before the farmer plows his own fields, which are separated by banks two or three feet high, water must be pumped into them from waterways and ditches. The water is allowed to stand for a few weeks to soften the hard, caked earth, and to rot weeds and grass. Throughout the long, hot day, the farmer and his eldest son pump water with a wooden wheel. The wheel is attached to a hub. Long, flat, wooden paddles, like the spokes of a wheel, push the water to the field. Extensions from the hub, with pedals on each side, turn in sockets. The farmer and his son, their feet on the pedals, push downward con-

tinuously to turn the wheel. They lean on a crossbar with their arms. A small roof of palm fronds furnishes a little shade if they are not lucky enough to be near a tree.

Later the water is drained off and the seed is sown in nursery beds. It comes up quickly, and soon patches of soft, bright green shoots, like velvety rugs, are scattered around the brown fields. Some of the fields are partly filled with water, muddy clods rising above the surface. Others reflect the sky above in blue or white squares.

While the seedlings are growing, the farmer prepares his other fields to receive them. Big, slate-colored buffaloes help with the work. One or two buffaloes are attached to a homemade plow and slowly plod through the mud. The plow is shaped of two pieces of lumber bound together at an angle. The longer piece of wood is attached to the animal's yoke, and the shorter one holds a metal plowshare which has been bought at the market. The farmer guides the plow by an upright attached to the end of the shorter timber.

The buffaloes look fierce, with wide horns four or more feet across, but a small child can handle them. They are only worked in the early morning and late afternoon, for they cannot stand much heat. They wallow in the shallow water when the sun is overhead. A small boy watches carefully so that they will not stray.

The buffalo is a valued friend and helper to the family. It is much mourned when it dies, but even after death it is still valuable. Its skin is used for hide; its big horns are sold to be made into combs, boxes, knife handles, and other items. The meat is usually given away to friends. The farmer's family will not eat it, nor profit from it, as they owe so much to the animal for its years of service.

When the fields are ready, the rice is transplanted and the water is kept at the proper level for the growing rice. As the grain begins to form ears, boys go out to watch it and protect it from predatory birds. Sitting on a rickety platform raised on stilts, the boys scare away the birds by shaking bamboo clappers or flapping their arms; sometimes they slap a wet lump of clay from the end of a swishy length of bamboo at sassy crows who become too daring. The boys happily chase away the family ducks and chickens which they would never dare chase at any other time.

When the fields have turned brown with the ripened grain, the plants are cut with a kind of sickle. The crop is spread in the sun for several days, and when dried, is bound into sheaves.

Two workers winnowing rice. The large woven basket contains kernels threshed from the heads of the rice.

The farmer puts his threshing ground in readiness while the crop dries. He pounds the earth with a wooden mallet, adding buffalo dung so that the surface will be hard when it dries. Sometime the farmer beats the sheaves against the ground to loosen the grain; sometimes several buffaloes, guided by a member of the farmer's family, tread around a central post over the rice straw.

After the grain is detached, it is tossed in the air from a flat basket to separate it from the chaff. If there is no breeze, the farmer uses a fan with a long handle.

The farmer who has only a few fields keeps his unhusked rice (called *paddy*) under the house in large baskets covered with flat, woven trays. The baskets stand on layers of rice straw which raises them above the ground. A larger harvest is kept in a dome-shaped, woven granary which is plastered with a layer of mud and buffalo dung, and covered with palm-leaf thatch to protect it from the weather. It is raised above the ground on a wooden platform.

The paddy is stored in the husks — the farmer's wife taking it out as she needs it and husking it herself. For husking, the grain is placed in a hollowed-out section of a tree trunk which is partially buried in the ground to hold it fast under the pounding blows of a long, lever-like wooden pestle. This method conserves some of the nutritious outer covering of the rice so that it is better than factory-milled grain. The farmer cooks the bran to feed to his animals.

Rice is served with every meal in Thailand by both the rich and the poor. Two meals a day are standard — one in the morning and one in the late afternoon — but nibbling goes on all day.

Small bowls of tea are served with the meal; sweets and fruits are eaten as between-meal snacks

The cooking is done on a red-clay stove shaped like a large flowerpot, with ridges at the top to hold a cooking vessel. There is a square hole in the side to furnish a draft for the charcoal smoldering inside on a grating. If there is a larger stove, it is made of clay and shaped like a horseshoe, with a grating across the top. The cook sits on the floor and scraps are swept through chinks between the boards to fowl waiting beneath the house. The kitchen is furnished with few utensils; there are knives, spoons, dippers of tin or coconut shell, a mortar, and a grater shaped like the wheel of a spur for shredding coconut or dried fish. There is a big, shallow iron bowl for frying, clay rice pots and water jars, and a padded basket to hold the teapot and keep it warm.

The rich have a greater variety of foods served in finer dishes. Many of the upper classes have adopted Western ways of eating and they can afford meat more often.

As the teachings of Buddha warn against taking the life of any creature, it may seem inconsistent that the Buddhist Thai catch fish and eat the flesh of animals. When Buddhism came to Thailand, the teachers found that the population ate quantities of fish and their diet would have been very meager without it. It is difficult to change the habits of an entire people.

Humans usually rationalize the things they want to do. The Thai say that the stupid fish enter the traps and nets. They are only taken from the water — they die and are not killed. And if an animal dies, what does it matter who

eats it? In this manner, the Thai explain away their dis-
obedience to the Buddhist commandment against killing
any living creature. Most Thai will not kill animals, and
they look down upon hunters. Killing animals seems a
much greater sin than fishing. Fish have only a feeble in-
telligence they say. It is a much more evil thing, the Thai
believe, to hunt down an animal, for an animal runs in
terror from its pursuer.

At one time the king forbade any hunting or fishing on
holydays. At certain festivals, rich men bought whole cargoes of fish and returned them to the water.

In the shallow waters of the Gulf, and in rivers and
streams, there are countless varieties of fish. The Thai use
them all. In the inland waterways, the peasant catches
fish for his food. If he has too much, he sells the surplus at
the market. The peasant makes many sorts of fish traps
and nets of bamboo and fibers. Even the paddy fields furnish fish. When the water rises, it carries the fish from the
streams into the flooded fields and ditches. In the wet
fields, before the rice is planted, fish are caught in nets
and basket scoops. Later, homemade lines and poles are
used, so that the rice may not be harmed.

In the evening, after his farm work is done, a man rows
his sampan out to a large net he has staked in the river.
The net is shaped rather like an umbrella, braced at the
top with four bamboo poles. Four more flexible poles are
attached to the corners and meet together, swinging from
a long arm fastened to the stake. The net is lowered into
the water, then raised when it contains fish. The smaller
nets are two yards across, but some are so large that they
must be raised by a windlass from docks along the shore.
These belong to commercial fisheries.

Another method of fishing is done by two people. They

haul a drag net between them, or stretch it between two boats, and pull the net through the water.

Along the coast, where the land is low, mud and sand flats stretch outwards to the horizon at low tide. Long piers reach towards the water, crowded with sun-baked huts and shacks. Beside them run rickety duckboards. Drying nets hang on racks like old, brown spider webs. Masts of ships that floated at high tide tilt at all angles alongside the piers. Sampans careen on their sides, attached to stakes in the mud, the surface of which is broken by occasional blue puddles.

The sea has deserted the land, looking as though it could never find its way back. But soon it slips stealthily towards shore, making runnels of water, filling puddles and pools, until it lifts the tired-looking boats again and they bob jauntily, slapped by the sparkling waves. Sails spread to the breeze and the boats start out to sea. They

A large drop net, braced by flexible bamboo poles, is maneuvered into the water by a fisherman and his wife.

head for the mouths of rivers and estuaries. Here long lines of poles converge to a large net that is stretched between other poles. The sluggish river and tides carry the fish between the rows of posts to the net. Further out, the brown, silty water forms a distinct line with the clear water of the Gulf. Chugging, smoky launches seem to pull a stream of muddy water in their wake, leaving a brown path in the blue water that indicates the way they have gone.

Further south the coast rises in hills and the Gulf is deeper. When the fishing boats sail out in the early morning, they are accompanied by men in sampans, paddling swiftly. When they reach a likely fishing ground, the sampans scatter around. A man dives overboard from each, into the clear water. Coming up now and then to breathe, he watches and listens for shoals of fish under the water. When he spots them, he surfaces and signals his boat.

The men in the fishing boat pay out a seine net in a large circle, then tug and strain to draw in their catch. Flocks of sea gulls shriek overhead, swooping down to look for a prize.

At noon it is time for the tired men to go home. They sail past the rough coast that is tangled with vegetation and edged with white beaches. A sweet smell blows from the land. The ships pass a steep island, a green cone of vegetation rising straight from the deep water. It is humming with insects.

When the men arrive at the port, they sell their catch to fish factories that are cluttered with pickling vats, salting pits, and drying racks. At the factories, gangs of women sort and gut the fish. Any fish that are too bony or small for eating, along with scraps and bits, are thrown into troughs. This conglomeration is pounded and kneaded, then left to dry partially. Salt is added. The mixture is packed in jars, or dried further, and pressed into flat cakes. It is sold in markets all around the country as a seasoning. It announces its presence by a strong and fishy odor, but the Thai do not object to the smell, and it is a favorite flavoring.

The Thai are fine sailors, managing their ships in all kinds of weather. Sudden storms and gales may lash the waves into the open boats and toss the fishing vessels about in the heavy seas. But fishing is important to the Thai. The sailors burn candles and incense on their boats to propitiate the wild spirits of the sea. On the fine, sunny days, the grateful sailors give thanks to the spirits who have granted a good catch.

4

Archaeology and Architecture

*"If you select the wrong site, you will regret it
until the building falls."*

Ruins of long-forgotten cities and temples can be found in
the forests of Thailand. Often there is no record of their
past nor of the busy people that inhabited them. Sites of
old cities have been built upon again and again; bricks
and stones have been carried away to be used in newer
buildings. Old temples were seldom repaired but were left
to crumble; more merit was gained by erecting a new one.

The principal towns and cities, like many fortified cities
of Europe, were fortresses. They had to be strong to withstand assault. Thai cities were surrounded by heavy walls,
sometimes one within another. In battle, thundering elephants charged at the walls, and hordes of armed men
strove to enter or camped outside for long sieges. The remains of these walls still stand, some forming the backs of
houses or shops. Sometimes it looks as though an entire
town is huddling against the walls.

Toward the end of the last century, King Chulalongkorn
became interested in Thailand's past. The jungle was ex-
plored and sights of old temples cleared of entangling
vegetation. Some monuments among the tumbled blocks
of stone were found to be fairly well preserved. There

were solid spires, columns that only supported the sky, and stairways that led to nothing. They were lichen-covered, matted with vines and ferns. Roots had slipped into crevices, slowly pushing the great stones apart, toppling them to the ground. Great roots of trees twisted about the mounds like giant boa constrictors petrified in the midst of a fierce struggle. Wooden palaces and houses and the timber roofs of temples had been eaten away by dampness, foliage, and termites.

Roots had to be hacked away carefully so that the carving beneath would not be injured. Accumulated silt was removed, revealing secrets that had been kept a long time in the silent forests. Stone walls had fallen, but solidly built *Phra Chedis* still stood. Surrounded by rubble, they pushed upward through the treetops towards the sky.

The word "Phra" in Thai is applied to many things. It means regal, sacred, exalted, or respected. It is placed before the titles of kings, applied to monks, and used before the venerated names of places and objects of religion. Phra Chedis are the most venerated of Thai monuments. They were derived from the mound, called a *stupa*, which was placed over the burial place of Buddha. They became symbols of religion and were erected to announce that the teachings of Buddha had come to a certain place. Even if small and plain, stupas were never torn down. Later, when a finer one was wanted, it was built around the old one. A Phra Chedi might contain a holy relic or be a copy of one which contained a relic of Buddha.

The Phra Chedis are not parts of buildings, but stand separately. Old and new, they are all around Thailand, six feet or hundreds of feet high. There are many variations on the basic design built in different periods and in different parts of the country. They are built on a base, called a *drum*, which is made of a series of steplike moldings, each less in circumference than the one below. The base may be round or square in outline. Sometimes it is niched in a number of indented angles at the corners. Above the base rises the *dome*, either bell-shaped, a flattened ball, or an elongated pyramid with slightly concave sides and a rounded top. Over this is the *umbrella*, a sign of honor, represented by diminishing disks or balls, and ending in a spire and a finial. Phra Chedis may be built of stone, solid cement masonry, or brick and earth covered with stucco. In later periods they were decorated with designs in stucco or flowery porcelain.

Another type of spire, called a *Phra Prang*, originated from the elongated, pointed dome of a Khmer temple, which covered the room of the sanctuary. It was reached by steep steps to several terraces, one above the other. The Phra Prang is now solid, on a base suggested by the terraces. Those of later periods are more elongated and slender than those of earlier ones. The great tower of Wat Arun at Bangkok is a Phra Prang.

Remains of temples of the Khmer period are found in central and northeastern Thailand. The Khmer temple was the temporary abode of a Hindu god, and had to be worthy of him. It symbolized the Brahman concept of the central mountain of the universe, called Phra Meru, where the gods dwelt. The central tower stood for the various heavens; the smaller, similarly shaped ones which surrounded it were rocky crags on the sides of the mountain; the doorways with arched and carved vestibules symbolized cave mouths which were guarded by mythological beings. Every surface was elaborately carved with designs and figures. There were celestial beings dressed in ancient court costume, there were demons, and many differ-

ent animals. The symbol of the air was the fierce Garuda,
called *krut* by the Thai. It is part bird, part man and has
outspread wings with hands. There are elephants that
represent the earth, and bulls and horses that stand for the
sun and fire. The Naga, or serpent, is prominent in Khmer
architecture; it symbolizes the waters and rain and also
the rainbow, stairway to heaven.

Later, under Buddhism, all these figures were kept to
indicate that the old gods acknowledged the teachings of
Buddha. There are also remains of Khmer Buddhist temples, built when the two religions were practiced together.
These temples are simpler in design, not built on high terraces, and contain only one story.

At Angkor, in Cambodia, there are the remains of a city,
and many temple ruins are in the area. The walled city
Angkor Thom once covered many square miles and had a
million inhabitants. Most of its two hundred massive monuments were built in the eleventh century. The magnificent city lasted four hundred years until it was conquered
by the Thai from Ayudhya and its riches carried away. In
a treaty drawn up in 1867, the Thai ceded Cambodia to
the French. The city of Angkor Thom and the temples,
overgrown with jungle, were discovered by the French.
They cleared much of the growth away and restored the
tumbled stones of buildings.

The largest of the Khmer temples is at Angkor, about a
mile from the city. It was dedicated to the gods Shiva and
Vishnu. The central tower above the sanctuary rises two
hundred and fifteen feet above the ground. Lesser towers
rise from three tall terraces, one above the other. The first
terrace is three hundred feet long at the base. The building
is indeed a mountain for the gods. The temple was once

served by thousands of people: priests and their assistants, officials, musicians, and dancing girls.

Steep steps, worn smooth by countless bare feet, rise
from one terrace to the next. Each terrace has four open
courts separated by vaulted-roofed passageways. The sun
filters through the openings in the carved stone sides.

A wide stone causeway crosses a moat six hundred feet
wide. The moat leads to the temple. It is now dry, but
once must have reflected the grandeur of the building.
When the surface of the water was disturbed by wind, the
sun's reflection must have quivered over the carved figures, making them pulse with life.

Everywhere there is intricate carving, but with no feeling of confusion. The masses of design are so well arranged that the attention is held by the main figures. Some
of the carvings are bold, others lacy.

On the walls of the base are long stone murals in high
relief depicting Hindu myths. The details are of historical
interest; they show not only the life of royalty of the
period but that of the common people as well. There are
hunting and battle scenes backed with luxuriant foliage. A
prince sits in his palace which is held up by Garudas to show
that it is floating in the air. He is surrounded by princesses
and dancing girls who wear tall, pointed crowns. Then he
is shown in a boat rowed by many oarsmen. The boat has
high curved ends similar to the ceremonial ones used centuries later. There are parasols and fans such as are seen
today. Myriads of fish swim in the water. There are scenes,
too, of blissful heavens and terrible hells.

In places vegetation still swarms over the stones. Trees
rise from the roofs of small shrines, huge roots flowing
down. Once small as a thread, now these roots are great,
twisted cables. The stone and roots appear to be as one;

a carved doorway seems to be the entrance to a dryad's
tree-home.

The fine-grained sandstone of Angkor held carving well,
but in the region around Sukhodaya the laterite blocks
used in building were unsuitable for carving. This material, soft and claylike when dug from the ground, hardens
on exposure to the air. Architectural details were added
with stucco made of sand, lime, and a glue made of soaked
buffalo hide and molasses. This mixture, also used as a

mortar, became hard as granite; it has lasted hundreds of years.

Designs were outlined in plaster on the surface of a wall. The portions in high relief were molded separately and stuck on later; the rest of the decorations were done directly on the wall. Door and window frames, balustrades, finials, and large figures were all made of stucco. They still are. When the old buildings fell, the stucco cracked with them, but many figure heads and large fragments of decorations were found in the ruins.

A difference in function, and in the materials used, brings a change in architecture. The narrow aisles and small enclosures of the Khmer could be made entirely of stone. The corbeled arches of their doorways were formed by stone blocks, stepped forward, resting one on the other, the arch smoothed inside. When assembly halls covered a large area in the Buddhist temples, the vaulted roof could not be used. Instead, temples were roofed with wood. Features derived from the Khmers were no longer an essential part of the structure. The central tower became decorative. Made of wood for lightness, it was high and slender, and mounted on a building where four roofs met together. In the later palaces and temples, steep timber roofs overlap one another, the lower ones projecting beneath the higher, similar to the temples built in the last centuries. These later temples can be seen today.

These roofs are covered with brilliantly-colored glazed tiles. Heavy stone Nagas, which decorated Khmer arched doorways, have become light and graceful wood carvings that edge the gable ends of these buildings. The Nagas seem to be draped over beam ends and are finished with a finial at the peak, curving like a slender horn. These decorations are covered with gold leaf. (A bit of gold, about the weight of a twenty-five-cent piece, is beaten into a thousand thin, two-inch sheets and used for gilding.)

The space enclosed by the gable ends and the curves of the Naga is approximately shaped like the outline of a seated Buddha, giving the observer a feeling of peace and happiness. The surface of this space contains designs in molded stucco, sometimes set with porcelain ornaments; or it is carved of wood, gilded, and set against a background of glass mosaic. The mosaic bits are made of very thin glass backed with colored metal foil, then cut into small pieces with scissors. Symbolic Buddhist or Brahman designs and figures are used among the conventional floral patterns, lotus, interlaced vegetation, or flowing shapes like floating streamers.

Columns with gilded capitals, developed from lotus forms, support the roof of the portico; or if there is a gallery all around the building, the wide overhanging eaves rest on many columns.

At the sides of the doorways there are pilasters. They appear to hold a superstructure made of stucco in high relief. It is shaped like a high, pointed crown, like the frosting on a wedding cake, or it may resemble a shallow gable end. The entire effect is somewhat baroque, but there is balance between the colors of tiles, the gilding and ornamentation, and the large white surfaces of the building — and all has great charm.

All of the structures grouped together within a wall are called collectively *wat*. There is a large building for monastic ceremonies, another where services are held for the congregation. In each there is a figure of Buddha on a high altar. There are Phra Chedis and Phra Prangs of various

sizes, and possibly a library and bell tower. There are open-roofed pavilions used for many purposes — for teaching or just for sitting in the shade and talking. These pavilions are shaded by trees. Mythological figures and ornamental shrubs in molded bases stand about on the stone-paved grounds. There are living quarters for the monks at one side. There may be a roofed colonnade containing rows of Buddhas against a background of a painted mural.

One temple building in Bangkok is on a terrace surrounded by a parapet. A series of panels on the building contains carvings in bas-relief on gray stone depicting events from a long tale of Thai mythology. As one looks up, one sees groups of boys holding thin papers in place. They are busily at work making rubbings from the stone panels with black or red chalk. Some ambitious children use crayons of many colors, varying them to suit their own taste and imagination. The children wander around the wat grounds, trying to sell rubbings to anyone who looks like a tourist. The best of the rubbings in monochrome are beautiful and are sold in Bangkok shops.

There are so many wats in Bangkok that they could not be described in all their variations. The most beautiful of all is Wat Phra Keo, which contains the king's temple. The boundaries are formed by cloisters with double orange roofs that are supported by gilded brackets. The wat has a solid wall on the outside. Inside there is an open colonnade containing rows of Buddha images. The entrance gates resemble small temples, and are guarded by giant-sized demons covered with porcelain.

A Phra Chedi which dates from about the fifth century.
It was originally an Indian stupa, or burial mound.

Among a small forest of Phra Chedis reflected in the marble pavement, one large monument towers over all the soaring roofs of buildings. Its surface is of gleaming gold covered over with glass tiles, and it startles one's eyes in the bright sunlight. It is the Pantheon which stands on a double terrace reached by flights of marble steps. It is flanked by golden Phra Chedis, with rows of outstretched Garudas at the base. The feathered arms of the Garudas seem to support them, symbolizing that they are air-borne.

The Pantheon consists of four wings, each with overlapping roofs. The wings are surmounted at their intersection by a tall tower shaped like a Prang, a purely decorative feature. Tiles of colored porcelain cover the walls and the tall columns that support the roofs. King's palaces were built in this style, and it is now used in temples, for the kings in the past often donated their palaces to a wat.

The kings received ambassadors in one of the great halls of the Pantheon. Next to it stands the royal temple. Not quite as lofty, it contains a small Buddha figure, the most revered one in the country. Inside and out, the wat is adorned with all the glory imagination could devise.

All about gold sparkles. White backgrounds glare; they are almost too bright in the sun. Porcelain garlands drip like jeweled necklaces. Everywhere there is something new to see in this fantastic place.

The architecture has a soaring lightness combined with solidity, designed "to hold together the heavens and the earth." Everything is full of the charm of the unexpected; it is rich, gleaming, magical, and entirely individual.

5

Buddhism, the Religion of the Thai

"At the end of life, the soul goes forth alone; only our good deeds will befriend us."

Most of the Thai have followed Buddhism for seven hundred years. The religion has spread to hundreds of millions of people around the world. It came to Thailand from Ceylon, and is the official religion. The word for Buddha derives from Sanskrit and means "the wise and enlightened." Gautama Buddha is said to be the fourth Buddha who has appeared on earth, and others will follow him.

The father of Gautama Buddha was a king in India in the sixth century B.C. When his son was born, the king was warned by seers that four things in the future would cause Gautama to renounce his royal life for a religious one. He would see an old man, a sick man, a corpse, and an ascetic. As the king wished his son to remain his heir, he gave orders to protect the boy from seeing these omens.

When he was sixteen, Gautama married and lived amid luxury and amusements in a fine palace his father had built for him. One day when he was out riding, he passed a very old, wrinkled man at the roadside. He asked why the man looked as he did. He was told that was the appearance of everyone who lived long enough. The prince pondered sadly that life was evil, leading only to the infirmity of old age. Later, when he had seen a man with a terrible disease, and a decaying corpse, it strengthened this feeling. Then he saw a holy hermit, and wondered if the true way of life was not asceticism. Gautama decided that the pleasures of life were not real. He was determined to leave the palace and seek solitude, where he would be able to meditate while trying to find the meaning of all things. A son had just been born to him, which made his ties with his old life even harder to break.

One night, while the court was sleeping, he quietly left the palace on his favorite horse. (There is a charming Thai painting of this episode. Angels have come to hold the hoofs of the horse so that they will not clatter on the court-yard tiles. The horse, with Gautama, seems to float over the palace wall, while the courtiers are shown sleeping soundly in their elaborate apartments.)

When far from the palace, Gautama changed his royal robes for those of the mendicant ascetic. He learned from holy men all that they could teach him, but it was not enough to answer his questions. He went to a quiet spot and sat under a bo tree for forty-nine days. At last he attained enlightenment; the perfect knowledge of the truth was revealed to him. He had reached the state of a Buddha. He could now be released from all earthly things. Deciding to forgo this peace, he went about preaching his laws for the good of humanity. He traveled and taught until the end of his long life, making many disciples whom he sent out to teach his laws.

During the rainy season it was difficult to travel, so Gautama retired to a monastery where he continued to instruct his disciples. (This period became the Buddhist Lent. The Thai name for this time is *Phansa*. It lasts for three months, starting in the middle of June. Many religious services are held and gifts are given to the wat. Everyone is expected to be especially devout. The monks live austerely and spend time in contemplation, and many new monks join the monastery during this period.)

Buddha became ill when he was eighty years old. He told his disciples that his time of deliverance was at hand, that he would soon pass to nirvana, the state of peace and freedom from the miseries of the constantly changing illusion which is existence.

Buddhism does not describe nirvana, for it is beyond human understanding. But it is said that anyone who achieves it "will be seen no more." It is through loss of desire, selfishness, evil, and illusion that this state of wisdom, holiness, and peace is reached.

Every act brings a consequence which passes on from one stage to the next. Good and evil deeds cause a better or worse stage. Life is an unending cycle of illusion which the ignorant mistake for reality. No living thing is permanent from moment to moment, but constantly passes through change, growth and decay, so individuality is only a figure of speech and an illusion.

To help mankind escape, Buddha stated four truths, called the *Wheel of the Law*: first, pain is caused by birth, sickness, old age, death, and by attaining things disliked and by not attaining those desired; second, that pain is produced by desire and longing for illusory satisfaction that is impossible to attain; third, perfect extinction of desire will destroy pain; and last, a pure heart and perfect conduct will cause the end of desire and bring the attainment of peace.

Buddha also left precepts for living: subdue hatred with love, overcome passions and anger, control the mind, give alms freely, neither steal nor practice deceit, and be kind to all living things. There are many more rules for the monastic orders, and they are stricter for the monks, who by precept and example, are supposed to lead in the effort against evil and illusion.

There are many levels of Buddhist belief among the Thai, from the simple peasant to the intellectual. Intellectual people revere Buddha as a great teacher and hope to keep his moral code. To them, temples, religious symbols, and statues of Buddha are reminders of the right way to live. Many Thai peasants and pious people with simple ways of thought find the philosophy of Buddhism hard to understand, so it is a comfort to them to think of Buddha as a deity to be worshiped and offered prayers. To them, a statue of Buddha is more than a reminder.

Old religious manuscripts contain many myths and stories of miraculous happenings in the life of Buddha. There are detailed descriptions of heavens and hells and of the cosmology of the universe, later additions to the teachings. The intelligent consider these tales as illustrative allegories, but the simple people think of them as realities. Many people today take the old legends as seriously as did people in former centuries.

The less educated do not look as far ahead as nirvana. They only plan for a better situation in the next life: to find temporary happiness in one of the many heavens, or to avoid the horrors of grim hells.

Buddha did not teach the existence of a god. When asked about the gods he said the question was an unprofitable one for there was no means of knowing the answer. As Buddhism has always been tolerant of other ways of religious thought, the old Hindu gods and ideas have also influenced the Thai.

To the Thai, Hell was filled with demons, and celestial beings lived in the heavens. These, with earth spirits, were all subject to the same laws of change as mankind. Some later writers claimed that these supernatural beings were converted to the Buddhist doctrine, and others that the beings are merely abstractions.

In the first centuries after Buddha attained nirvana, it would have been a sacrilegious act to make a representation of the Master. Symbols were used instead, to remind his followers of his life and teachings. In early carvings Buddha is not seen, symbols indicate he is there. They represent the great events of his life. He sat beneath a bo tree to meditate, so a slablike seat or a tree represents the meditation and enlightenment. A decorative wheel, sometimes with deer as supports, indicates the time when Buddha first preached in the deer park near Benares, thus, according to Buddhist doctrine, "setting the Wheel of the

Law in motion." A footprint is a reminder of Buddha's travels from place to place as he spread his teachings. The symbol of his entrance to nirvana at his death is a stupa, or funeral mound. These signs may be more or less elaborately designed.

These subjects keep recurring in the art of the country. When Buddha was finally represented, the symbols became the backgrounds of bas-reliefs and paintings.

Sometimes Buddha is pictured surrounded by disciples. Sometimes scenes from his life are shown. Solid figures of Buddha are the most important subject in Thai sculpture. These statues were made in the thousands, and many date back to the sixth century A.D. The early ones were carved in stone. From the thirteenth century on they were also cast in bronze. Through the centuries, variations of design arose, but it is difficult to date the figures exactly. Artists copied figures of preceding generations, and the essential characteristics of Buddha have been preserved.

The classic description of Buddha's appearance was laid down long after his death: *The Buddha's image has broad shoulders, his arms are long and rounded, like the trunk of an elephant, and his hands and fingers taper like the petals of an opening lotus. His legs are like the round, smooth stems of banana trees, and the soles of his feet are flat. His head is like an egg, with a chin like a mango seed; his brows arch like drawn bows; his ears are long to show nobility; and his curls turn in the direction of the sun's path. His expression is calm and serene.*

His robe is indicated by a few lines to show the folds. It is seen with difficulty, representing the fact that his body shone with his fiery energy. When standing or walking, the body is placed against the folds of his garments. An aura is indicated with gilding or with a circle of flames

*The focal point of this temple is the elaborate sitting
Buddha of the Sukhodaya school — 14th or 15th century.*

around his body. The finial on top of the figure's head in
early examples, looks like a small mound of Buddha's hair.
Later it became more stylized, until today it is represented
as a flame.

Occasionally Buddha is shown wearing princely attire
with a conventionalized design of jewels around his neck.
In the late Bangkok period, the decorative designs of
jewels were so exaggerated that they covered the whole
figure and included an elaborate crown. It is a decadent
style, and simplicity of design is lost. In some periods
Buddha's fingers are all of the same length, in others they

vary. In the standing figures there are some differences in the flow of the garments.

Buddha is shown in four postures — standing, walking, sitting, and reclining — and there are twelve usual gestures of the hands. In the standing figures, the hands held shoulder-high, palms outward, show exposition or teaching. When Buddha dispels fear, both hands may be held outwards at elbow height, or one may hang down at his side.

The sitting figure shows Buddha in meditation, one leg folded above the other, soles upwards. One hand rests in his lap and the other on his right knee. He sits on many varieties of pedestals: a conventional lotus, or a series of ornamental steps that taper to the top. Sometimes he sits on the coils of a Naga, a serpent, done more or less realistically.

There is a story that once, when Buddha sat in meditation, oblivious to everything around him, a great storm broke. Heavy rains flooded the land. A Naga saw that Buddha was in danger from the rising waters. He did not want to disturb the Master's thoughts, so he slipped his coils, with great care, beneath Buddha and raised him above the flood. Then the Naga spread his seven-headed hood above Buddha to shield him from the rain. This incident is often depicted.

Not many statues were made in the Bangkok period. Wars had left many old ruins at Ayudhya and other places containing images of Buddha. These statues were rescued and installed in temples wherever they were needed. Many extra figures were placed in rows in the open cloisters around monastery courts. When work on statues was again started, the old classic rules were neglected, and the statues did not have the beauty of the earlier examples.

One of the most famous statues of Buddha in Thailand is the one popularly called the Emerald Buddha. It is in the Royal temple at Bangkok. The statue is looked upon as the protector of Thailand and its kings. Thirty-one inches high, it is carved of green, translucent jasper and rests on a gilded throne inside an open pavilion. The top of the pedestal is thirty-four feet above ground, so it is difficult to see the statue well. This Buddha image is thought to have come from Ceylon originally. It has followed the fortunes of war, becoming the property of the

Detail from the porcelain tiling used on a wat building.
The background is yellow; red predominates in the design.

conquerors. It was captured by the Thai of Ayudhya from the city of Chiengmai in 1641.

The Emerald Buddha's robes are changed three times a year by the king himself, who climbs steps placed before the high altar. In the cold season the robe is of gold embroidered cloth encrusted with jewels, draped rather like a stiff shawl. In the hot, dry season the garment is made of gold net, and in the wet season, the Buddhist Lent, it is of the same yellow cloth the monks wear.

Reclining figures of Buddha represent his last days and his entrance into nirvana. He lies on his side, his head supported by one hand, the other hand flat along the upper side of his body. The legs are straight, one foot above the other, showing the flat soles of his feet.

A figure of a reclining Buddha in Bangkok is one hundred and fifty feet long and lies on a high pedestal in a long, narrow building. The statue's big, pearly eyes look down blindly. The top of the head, near the painted roof, is forty feet from the ground. The foundation of the figure is brick, covered with plaster and finished with gold lacquer. Before it was regilded, it had weathered to a golden brown with the years of wreathing smoke. The smoke came from incense and candles which had been placed on an iron rail surrounding the pedestal by those who wished to pay homage. Hundreds of small, gleaming squares of gold leaf were scattered about the surface of the statue by the pious in an attempt to keep the surface golden.

Even though the surface has been regilded and does not need these offerings, people still wish to carry on the tradition. There are several small altars placed by the pedestal containing three-foot-long replicas of the large Buddha. The offerings are made to these. The tissue thin, one-and-a-quarter inch squares of gold leaf can be bought at the temple for a small coin. The small figures are covered with these gold squares, the corners of which come loose and flutter in the slightest breeze, giving the images an elusive, uncertain surface and an air of unreality. The facing seems to be covered with small flames, showing the "fiery energy" of Buddha.

The feet of the main image are twenty feet long, and

Four Phra Prangs surround Bangkok's Temple of Dawn.
One of these elegant towers can be seen on the right.

the beautiful soles are covered with designs inlaid with pearl shell. All the toes are of the same length, the pads covered with intricate whorls.

In the center of the sole is a large diagram of the Wheel of the Law. Around it, in rectangles, are the one hundred and eight signs of the upper heavens, the stars, the planets, and continents and rivers of earth as conceived in mythology. There are animals, crowns and regalia of kings, lotus, and a monk's alms bowl. These are all beneath the feet of Buddha, signifying his superiority to all things.

According to legend, wherever a footprint of Buddha was found, the religion would flourish. Four footprints have been found in Thailand. Some say that Buddha has been there, others that his teachings have reached the spot. The footprints are large, natural hollows in rock that have been touched up by the pious.

The earliest religion in the region of Thailand was spirit worship. Spirits of nature and the elements were thought to be everywhere. Although Buddha warned his followers against superstition as an illusion, some of the spirits remain real to many Thai. Buddhism could not banish the spirits entirely from popular belief, nor could it dispose of the mythology of the Brahman religion that was adopted from the Khmer period.

Indian traders came to Cambodia, the country of the Khmers, in the early centuries A.D. They settled and brought their religion — Brahmanism — with them. They intermarried with the Khmers, who adopted the superior culture of the Indians. When Buddhism was brought to the country, it spread and flourished along with Brahmanism. There was never any hostility between the two religions. Sometimes the monarch or the people might have a preference for one, or both might be practiced together.

Buddhism did not designate any religious rites, but taught of spiritual things. So, for the ceremonies of life, either individual or public affairs, both the king and the people accepted the ancient Brahman ones. Brahman priests still officiate at these rites in Thailand, and Buddhist monks are not forbidden by the rules of their order to be present and to give a blessing to the occasion.

The Brahman gods became "kindly dwellers in the celestial heights." In their Thai versions they dwell in Mount Meru, the center of a complicated universe, and in the heavens about it. They represent abstract principles and the essence of nature and are believers in the teachings of Buddha. Each has special characteristics, and has an animal as a favorite mount. Indra is considered the protector of the earth and everything in it. He is shown riding a three-headed elephant. Vishnu rides a Garuda, king of the birds. Siva rides a white bull. And Brahma, a swan. The goddess Sarasvati rides a peacock.

She has four arms. In one hand she holds a lotus; she plays a musical instrument with two others. Ganesa has an elephant's head on a human body. The gods are often depicted with many arms, holding symbols of their qualities, or with different heads representing their different aspects.

All of these Brahman ideas, along with legends and old Buddhist tales, have influenced the art of Thailand. Wall carvings, statuary, painting, and architectural design primarily stemmed from religious thought. Much of it was made for the temple and wat buildings. When a demon statue guards a gateway, he is said to have been tamed by Buddha's teachings and to wish to mend his ways. Celestial beings, along with other legendary figures, were thought to have come to offer homage to Buddha. These mix with Buddhist symbols and nature forms.

All these art forms are intended to lead to a good way of life, whether revered as reminders or worshiped with pious simplicity.

In Thailand, people have never been persecuted for their beliefs. Tolerance is an essential part of Buddhism. In 1870, when King Chulalongkorn came to the throne, he stated in a royal proclamation: "Seeking and holding a religion that shall be a refuge for you in this life is a good concern. Every individual should investigate and judge for himself according to his wisdom, then hold it with all his heart, not with a shallow mind or from traditional custom. Follow its teachings and it will be a source of prosperity for all of you." And the Thai still hold to this way of thinking.

6

Life at the Wat

"As the immense sea contains the savor of salt, so the doctrine is saturated with the savor of deliverance."

A Phra Chedi can usually be seen from anywhere in Thailand, pointing to heaven above distant trees, reflected in the water of canals or in flooded rice fields. In the plains, wats rise like islands on raised ground in the fields. Low walls enclose them, and they are sheltered by trees. Hills are crowned with wats, and nearly every small village has one. The name "wat" includes all the buildings within the enclosure.

The wat holds an important place in the life of the country, and not only for its religious influence. Its carved and tiled buildings give pleasure to villagers who come to admire their beauty. People use wat grounds as a meeting place; travelers may stay overnight in its *salas*, which are open pavilions with templelike roofs resting on pillars. Those who sleep there must be careful that their feet do not point toward the figure of Buddha in the temple. The wat enclosure is an art gallery, town hall, clubhouse, and playground. Entertainments take place there on special occasions. It has the air of a cheerful park shaded by buildings, Phra Chedis, and trees. The largest of the trees in the wat is the bo tree which has trunks and roots twisted together and a mass of drooping branches with dark green leaves. All the bo trees in Thailand are said to have grown from a slip brought from Ceylon long ago. The bo tree is revered because Buddha sat beneath one when he attained enlightenment.

A drum or gong hanging in a tower is struck at eleven o'clock each morning, announcing the hour for the monks' last meal of the day. It also tells the time to the villagers.

The gnarled and twisted bo tree is revered in Thailand
as the tree beneath which Buddha attained enlightenment.

Government and local notices are posted in the wat, and people may gather to hear the news on the abbot's radio. The abbot dispenses charity to the needy and has funds from which he can lend small sums without interest. An educated man, the abbot is always ready to be consulted about anyone's problems. He must set a good example to all, and is the most respected person in the village. He presides over meetings of the townspeople as they discuss and vote on village affairs.

Lustral water is used in most ceremonies for purification and blessing. After a cremation it is sprinkled around the house in which someone has died, and anyone who has touched the corpse dips his hands in the water to purify them. At a wedding it is poured on the young couple by the guests and relatives. Lustral water is thought to avert trouble, disease, and danger. When it is being made holy, a candle is placed on the edge of a bowl of clean water. The bowl is passed along a row of monks who chant prayers as the wax drips into the bowl.

The monks hold their religious ceremonies in one temple building, while another is for the congregation. The buildings are large and rectangular, consisting of a nave, with or without side aisles. Round or square columns, made of large tree trunks or brick covered with plaster, support the roofs. The ceilings, walls, and columns are painted with designs, the colors softened by age and the smoke of candles and incense.

At one end of the temple building is a highly ornamented pedestal like an altar. On it sits a figure of the serene Buddha. Over his head is a many-tiered umbrella, symbol of sacredness and royalty. On the altar in front of the Buddha there may be a group of figures representing his disciples, and the votive offerings.

*While the monks sit on the floor, the wat's abbot
sits on a decorative bench, his fan by his side.*

On the floor in front are porcelain jars for flowers, large candlesticks holding huge candles, and bronze jars of sand into which those taking part in a service can place offerings of candles and incense sticks.

The only seat in the temple is a high bench for the abbot. Everyone else sits on a floor made of marble tiles or other stone. The monks sit with their legs folded in the manner of Buddha's image; the people sit with their legs to one side, a position of respect.

The monks live in cells in the wat compound. These are small rooms, often in a row under one roof. Each has a porch in front. The cells contain little, as the monks are dedicated to a life of austerity. There is a small altar with a figure of Buddha, a sleeping mat rolled up with bedding, a bamboo pole across a corner for clothing, and a cupboard. There is a lamp or candlestick. Outside, on the porch, stand two water jars that catch rain from the eaves. The monk's drinking cup is covered by a cloth strainer so that as he drinks he may not inadvertently take the life of anything that may be in the water.

He is served by a boy called a *dek-wat* (literally "boy-wat"). The boy sleeps on the porch before the monk's cell. He is usually ten to fifteen years old and does not wear any distinctive garb. The boy and his family both gain merit when he takes up the service of the monk. The boy can leave the service any time he wishes. He cleans up the cell, washes the monk's garments, and carries the monk's bag, umbrella, or fan when he accompanies the monk from the wat. The boy also carries money, for the monk is not supposed to handle currency. The dek-wat receives religious education at the wat, and he must also have time off to attend the government school.

Each monk wears open sandals, an undercloth which he keeps on for bathing, and a bright, saffron-yellow cloth draped about his body. The cloth, ten feet long by six feet wide, is something like a toga. It is redyed every three months by the dek-wat.

Each monk has an outer robe, also of rectangular shape, which he often wears folded and across one shoulder. It is made of many pieces of cloth sewn together and is symbolic of the early days of Buddhism when the monks were itinerant mendicants who dressed in castoff rags. The cloth is a reminder of humility. In former times, the robes were often discarded wrappings from the dead, picked up at the cremation site. Today, new cloth, which has been put over the coffin, is given to the monks who have chanted the funeral prayers.

Every two weeks the monk's head is shaved and the hairs of his eyebrows plucked out. He needs a parasol to keep his head cool when he walks in the hot sun. The monk's fan is not used to keep the air in motion, but is held in front of his face while he concentrates on holy thoughts. Some fans are very beautiful, embroidered with gold and silver thread and shaped like the spade in a pack of cards with a long handle. The fans have various designs, indicating the grade of the monk — from novice to patriarch. When the king wishes to honor a man, he bestows upon him a gold-and-enameled order. But a monk cannot accept such a gift, so instead the king honors him with a fan embroidered with the same design.

The monk rises early, about five o'clock. According to the rules for the monkhood he rises "as soon as he can see the veins in his hands." He washes, says a prayer in his cell, and then starts out. Carrying his alms bowl, he walks on a round of the town or countryside to collect his food.

The monk walks quietly with downcast eyes. He does not look up when a householder fills the bowl with food, nor does he give thanks. He must feel indifference and not consider what is given him.

When the monks return to the wat, they chant a blessing for the donors before they eat. If not enough food is given them for the two meals of the day, the temple boys cook more from the wat stores. They boil water for tea. After twelve noon nothing is eaten, but the monks may drink tea and liquids at any time. If there is any food left over it is fed to the dogs, cats, and birds that hang about the wats. Extra rice is spread to dry in the sun.

It is meritorious to donate rice at any time. After the harvest, when the farmer has the most rice on hand and so feels generous, a special festival takes place. It is called making a rice *chedi*. A woven fence is erected in the wat grounds; colored paper streamers flutter from tall bamboo poles at the corners. As each farmer pours his unhusked grain onto the growing heap, he holds a stick of incense and says a prayer, asking for a good crop in the coming year. He sticks a small paper flag in the gaily bristling heap. The wat will have a good supply for its storage bins.

A monk's day consists of many periods of prayer. He repeats a confession of sins, studies Buddhist lore, and teaches the temple boys and novices. One monk keeps account of the wat finances; another of the monks and novices that come and go. The monks see that the wat property is kept in good condition. They go out to conduct ceremonies for the people: invoking blessings at a marriage or birthday or housewarming celebration, chanting appropriate religious texts, providing lustral water for holydays and festivals, and carrying out the cremation rites.

There are many young, temporary novice monks attached to the wat. They enter for a few days upon the death of an older relative. Sometimes they stay much longer, usually for the months of the Buddhist Lent, thus making merit for themselves or their families and insuring a better condition in the future life. Their mothers and sisters, who do not have such an opportunity, are helped by this, too. It is considered ideal for every young man to join the monastery for some time, and possibly about half of them do. These novices wear the same yellow robes as the monks, but do not wear the cloth folded over one shoulder.

If he wishes to become a permanent novice and then a

monk, a man studies Pali (the language in which the sacred texts are written), the history of Buddhism, and the religious laws and scriptures. Then he must pass an examination.

The ritual is elaborate when a novice becomes a full monk. There is no ritual at all if a man joins the monastery for a very short time. Monks and novices may both leave the monastic life at any time and go back to the world or to another wat.

The rules of living for a monk are much more numerous and rigid than those for the novices and laity. He attempts to keep the 227 rules laid down for conduct, but it is understood that this is an impossible standard of virtue. If a monk breaks the most important rules, he is expelled from the order; less sins he must confess in person. For the minor ones, the monks all make a general confession once a year. Some of the rules forbid striking animals; going in a boat rowed by a woman; speaking while eating; and cultivating earth, lest an insect or worm be killed. He must not sit on any seat higher than twelve inches — as a sign of humility. (This rule does not apply to the abbot at a wat service.) He must not wear flowers behind his ears, play musical instruments, or enter a home uninvited.

Though a monk may not leave the wat overnight during Lent, at other times he may travel around the country. In fact, it is meritorious to visit holy shrines, but a monk must not stay at one place more than three days. If he lives in a monastery far from his home village, he may return there for some important religious ceremony with permission from the abbot.

Two monks and a girl show reverence out-of-doors to a Buddha sheltered in an ornamental stucco niche.

The monk travels along the roads or raised bunds between the rice fields with his alms bowl slung in a cloth. He is followed at a respectable distance by his dek-wat. The boy carries a large umbrella, the fan in a cloth-covered case, and a few necessary items in a woven cloth bag.

If there is no monastery in which to stay overnight, the boy raises the umbrella. It is as large as a beach umbrella. He plants it firmly in the ground, then drapes a white cotton cloth around it, making a small sheltering tent in which the monk sleeps. The boy sleeps wrapped in a cloth, even if the night is warm, as protection from mosquitoes. He would not dare to slap at a venturesome mosquito with his master so nearby.

When the sky flushes with the first glow of morning, they arise and continue on their silent way, stopping to collect food from any reverent household they pass.

7

The Thai Work with Metal

*"Do not barter gems for beads, nor a silver bowl
for an iron pot."*

Thai craftsmen have been skillful metalworkers since ancient times. Fortunately metals withstand the ravages of
time, so many things made of bronze and precious metals
have survived from former centuries.

There are cast-bronze figures of Brahman gods and god-
desses, heavenly beings, and mythological animals. There
are ceremonial utensils, fittings for chariots and palanquins, household and temple vessels of silver or gold, and
great bronze water bowls three feet high that once held
bath water. There are weights, used until recently in the
north of Thailand, to be placed on one side of a balance
scale that are shaped like conventionalized animals: elephants, lions, and birds, varying from the size of a pea to
several inches high.

Thousands of figures of Buddha have been found in ruins
or in old temples all about the country. There may be a
slight film of gilding left on the metal and the greenish
patina left by time. The old figures of Buddha often were
made of many metals fused together because the devout
who wished to partake of the merit of the casting used to
throw vessels of silver or bracelets and necklaces of gold

into the melting pot. These gifts were said to be for the Buddha's heart.

Buddha figures are still made today by the old methods. Large figures, some many yards high, have a core of clay· This clay core is covered with a wax surface of the thickness of the metal coating desired. The wax is worked into the shape and details of the figure, then it is embedded in a second mass of clay. Clay core, wax, and outside coating of clay are fired together in a kiln and the clay turns to

This bronze statuette of Buddha was found in one of the temple ruins. It is thought to be from the 13th century.

hard terra cotta. During the baking the wax runs out, leaving a space between the outer and inner molds.

Several workers prepare the metal in pots made of clay with an iron coating. The pots hang on a tripod over a teakwood fire, which gives a fierce heat. The clay mold of the figure is turned upside down and fixed firmly so it will be steady. Each worker pours molten metal from his pot into the space left by the wax.

When the image has cooled, the outer clay is chipped away. Then the figure is ready for finishing touches and polishing. For very large images, the flame on the head, the decorations, or the crowns are cast separately and attached later.

When the bronze is polished, it glows in various hues, from warm coppery tints to golden brass, for the Thai vary the alloys of copper, lead, tin, and zinc.

At one time special ceremonies had to be observed when a statue of Buddha was made. Work had to be started in the morning — the time when Buddha was born.

Four screens of white cloth were placed around the workers to keep away any sacrilegious onlookers and to block ill luck from entering. Monks sat outside, chanting prayers for the success of the undertaking.

Large and small bronze bells, some taller than a man, are cast for the temples. They hang in spired bell towers, or from stout beams. Long after the beam has rotted away the bells can be found on the ground where they have fallen. They do not have clappers but are sounded with sticks struck against their sides. They boom at eleven o'clock every morning, telling the time to temple dwellers and villagers.

There are gongs of many sizes. Some are musical instruments, some hang between a pair of elephant tusks and are struck with a padded stick to summon servants. Gongs were once carried into battle; the leader sent messages to his troops with their clanging.

Thai soldiers once carried round leather shields, bossed with metal, and long-handled, curved swords which they wielded with both hands. Some carried spears six to ten feet long with saberlike blades for slashing at the enemy. Some spears had long or short arrow-shaped blades, or a three-pronged head like a trident. All the weapons were made of untempered metal.

The blades of the nobles' swords were inlaid with designs in gold. The hilts were made of carved ivory or worked silver and decorated with red tassels; sometimes

Bellmakers in a small foundry in Thailand carefully shape the clay models from which bronze bells are cast.

silver wire was twisted around the hilts in intricate patterns.

Later there were firearms. Cannons were carried on the backs of elephants, the larger cannon were mounted on wheeled gun carriages and dragged into place.

An old manuscript, dated 1454, mentions gun foundries, and tells how to mix gunpowder and how to make incendiary rockets. It is believed that the earliest cannon did not fire shot, but threw out flames with loud explosions. This was often enough to stampede elephants and to put foot soldiers to rout. Some of the powder was designed to give so much smoke that the day became dim, adding to the confusion.

The earliest cannon were made of bronze. Then some Chinese ironmakers came to Thailand to make huge iron cauldrons. The reigning king noticed their work and decided that iron cannons could be made in much the same way.

A desolate spot shows where an old seventeenth century foundry once stood. The burnt earth is barren; shards of old iron lie partly buried among scanty weeds; slag clings to broken bits of pots in which metal was once melted. The area is surrounded by crumbling brick walls.

Some people say that the ghost of a Chinese gunmaker walks in this forbidding place. He was master of the foundry at the time when it was flourishing. He received an order to cast three cannons. After the first two were made, there was trouble with the third. The metal would not flow evenly into the mold, in spite of sacrifices offered to the spirits. Finally, the gunmaker offered his own life to the cannon spirits if the next time the metal was poured it would be successful.

With what mixed feelings he must have watched the

work! He would lose, whatever happened. This time the work went well. The molds were broken, the cannons polished, and they were ready to be shot for testing. When it came time to fire the third cannon, the Chinese foundry master stood in front of its muzzle in order to fulfill his vow. And, the story tersely ends, "he was seen no more."

Old cannons bear inscriptions engraved on the barrel. Some are marks which tell the caliber and the amount of powder needed for the charge, others the name of the maker and the day of casting. A typical inscription found on one old barrel reads:

"Ku commenced to cast on the thirteenth day of the waxing moon in the year of the Monkey, the last of small cycle, at two hours after sunrise."

The year corresponds to 1728 A.D.

Like battleships the world over, the cannons also had names engraved on them. The names alone might frighten an enemy! *"The Demon that Rends and Devours," "The Destroyer of the Earth,"* and *"The Eagle that Swallows an Elephant."*

The cannons were often decorated with inlaid designs in silver. A pair of these, made at the best foundry in Thailand, was sent to Louis XIV by King Narai when a French ambassador visited his court in 1685. The cannon were six feet long, with decorated barrels and carriages. Carlyle, in his *History of the French Revolution*, tells how they were dragged out to take part in the storming of the Bastille.

Metal for weapons came from the mines of Thailand where there are deposits of copper, tin, silver, and iron.

Steel sheets and galvanized iron are exported, but

enough stays behind to make ugly roofs for sheds and factories in place of the usual thatch or tiles. The roofs' gray color softens through the years, rusting to an uneven brown.

Iron is cast into everyday articles — plowshares, bowls, cooking vessels that will last twenty years, alms bowls for the monks. The last are made out of iron according to tradition and indicate the bearer's humility, although in the monastery the bowls may be kept within highly ornamental coverings.

Many things are made of galvanized iron and tin. In small shops workers sell their own goods. Sitting on the floor, they cut the metal into the required shapes with heavy shears whose big, looped handles are like butterfly wings. The street outside is filled with the noise of smiths' banging as they hammer out shapes on low anvils. Later these shapes are riveted or soldered to form buckets, pans, piping, gutters, water pots, and containers.

For centuries the Thai have made household knives of bronze. The knives hold a sharp edge very well. Today factories turn out handsome bronze tableware: not only knives, but also forks and spoons in Western style, with decorated handles of bronze, silver, or polished buffalo horn. These are displayed in shops beside brass bowls, vases, and trays, all engraved with Thai designs. And there are also candlesticks — some three feet high — made to hold huge candles similar to those in the temples.

Behind the fine shop, with its polished floors and glass display case, is a narrow, dusty warren of alleys. It is here that the beautiful objects in the display cases were made. The alleys are filled with large sheds. The sheds are dim, and inside sunlight filters down dustily through the cracks in the roof.

This gold repoussé plaque of a standing Buddha is from the Ayudhya period and was found in the Angkor Wat ruins.

Around the workers, on the floor, are baskets of partially-finished metalware. Ugly, long buffalo horns, dark gray with a rough, scored surface, are scattered about. The horns do not look as though they could ever be polished long enough to produce the lustrous, pearly surface of the finished knife handles which are lying nearby.

Long belts whir, turning polishing wheels for the metal and horn. A man sits beside an electric lathe, grinding decorative grooves into the handles. Shiny metal dust piles up like fairy gold on the floor. Nearby, another worker turns a heavy hand drill as he makes holes in the cutlery for the rivets that hold the handles in place.

The workers spend nine hours a day in these sheds, stopping at times to take a drink from the big, clay water jar, or to buy food from a passing vendor woman.

Next door to the bronze shed there may be one specializing in gold and silver. Gold is not mined in modern Thailand, although some is still found in the sands of many streams. It hardly pays to wash it out, but there must have been quantities of gold at one time. India, long ago, called Thailand "The Land Of Gold." The kings of Thailand used to send messages engraved on sheets of gold when they communicated with people of consequence. They did not sign the sheets for everyone knew that only the king could use gold for correspondence.

The kings' household articles were made of gold, too: betel sets, trays, washing and eating bowls, dishes and teapots, as well as the crowns, regalia, and jewelry.

All the wealthy people were covered with jewelry. Heavy earrings pulled down the lobes of their ears; gem-studded bracelets covered their arms; around their necks were necklaces, some supporting large flat plaques, embossed and jeweled. Anklets clanked above their feet — open circlets, the ends finished with decorative knobs, so they could be slipped easily around the legs.

Babies and very small children wore no clothes, but were bedecked with ornaments. They jingled as they ran about. The little girls wore heart-shaped silver plaques hanging from a loose chain around their waists. The children's skins were dusted with yellow saffron powder, which smelled aromatic and was believed to be cooling.

Boys and girls all had their heads shaved except for a twist of hair at the top of the head, through which an ornamental pin was thrust. This twist was shaved when they "came of age" at about nine years old. Many ceremonies accompanied this shaving, and then the hair was allowed to grow again. This custom lasted well into the present century.

Before the establishment of banks, jewelry was a way to keep wealth in a portable form, as well as a matter of prestige. Many peasant women still think it is the safest way to invest their money. In modern Thailand, men and boys do not wear jewelry.

Today, the goldsmiths and silversmiths still work at their crafts. One of the ancient arts that is still carried on is the making of niello. Patterns are hammered or etched with acid into a foundation, then the depressions are filled with a mixture of lead, copper, and silver forming a surface like black enamel. The finished piece has a delicate silver pattern on a highly-polished, jet-black ground. Sometimes the foundation may be of gold, sometimes the patterns are gilded.

Many things are made of niello: vases, bowls, dishes, ash trays, cigarette cases and lighters, and especially jewelry — necklaces, bracelets, and brooches — all bearing Thai designs.

In the workshop, men sit at small tables, busy at some part of the process. Ringing blows on metal strike out various overlapping rhythms: some slow and heavy as a man hammers out the silver forms on a wooden anvil, some lighter and quicker as other workers tap away, indenting surface patterns.

When the designs are finished, a stick of the black "enamel" is heated with a small electric blowtorch, dropping red-hot, melted pellets onto the surface. The pellets are smoothed into place with a blunt metal tool. The object is again heated to fuse the mixture with the silver, then it is set aside to cool.

The surface is filed down, removing all the black from the higher parts of the design. Now the surface is polished against the edges of heavy cotton cloth disks on a rapidly spinning electric wheel until the surface is shining and glossy. Old work is not as shiny as the modern for all the polishing was once done by hand.

The object is now ready to go to the shops of Bangkok or to be exported to many foreign countries.

Silver *repoussé* work does not take as much time. The patterns are drawn on the surface, then hammered from the inside against a mat of thick felt until they stand out in relief. Silversmiths have copied the old ornamental designs adapting them to new shapes: sugar bowls, creamers, candy dishes, napkin rings, boxes, buckles, and jewelry.

Modern copies of old Thai coins are sold for buttons and cuff links. The old coins were made of small, oval bars of silver, bent until the ends almost touched, leaving a small

12 inches

space between them. They looked like tiny, rolled-up arma-
dillos; in fact, the Thai called them "curled worms." The
coins could be carried strung together. The silver coins
were stamped on the convex top with the symbol of the
reigning monarch: an elephant; a Garuda, the man-bird;
or a lotus, simplified and conventionalized. The king's portrait was never used. It was considered part of him and so
might not be exposed to disrespect in the common market
place. These coins were in use until the middle of the last
century together with cowrie shells.

About eight hundred of the shells were worth a piece of
silver currency. They were brought by traders from India
and sold to Thailand. The king took a percentage and the
cowries filled huge jars in the treasury.

More and more currency was needed as the trades and

industry of Thailand grew. It became more convenient to make flat coins based on the decimal system. In 1880, King Chulalongkorn allowed his portrait to be used on coins — one of his many innovations. Flat coins are now standard, and the day of the "curled worms" is over.

Coins, household utensils, weapons of war, farm implements, religious artifacts, royal ornaments, jewelry — the ability of the metal craftsmen extends into all areas of Thai life. The functional and the decorative blend without friction.

In ancient times, the work was all hand done. Today, more and more, the simpler designs are being turned out by machines. But the beauty of the Thai design is not compromised by large-scale production. And there are always new metalworkers being trained in the old arts.

8

The Thai Make Pictures

*"What you have drawn with your hands, do not
erase with your feet."*

By the end of the nineteenth century the art of traditional
Thai painting had declined. With the influence of Western
art, an attempt was made to use perspective and shading
combined with the old forms instead of just the flat colors
and outlines that were used in the older Thai murals.
Many bright colors took the place of the softer hues of
earth colors. The work no longer showed the old vigor
and it seemed to have lost the capacity for growth.

The University of Fine Arts in Bangkok has revived the
techniques and traditions of the classical Thai arts and
painting, and teaches them along with contemporary
Western art. Many of the students are more interested in
learning the new ways, for they give more scope for individual expression than the old strict rules of traditional
painting allowed.

Modern Thai painters use a variety of techniques and
mediums. Much of their work is pleasing and competent,
with good design and color and many types of subject
matter, including Thai people and scenes. The work is
shown at an annual exhibition in Bangkok and also in
international exhibitions.

Some of the graduates of the University restore or copy old, damaged Thai murals before the work fades away forever, destroyed by the heat and dampness of the climate. Roofs of some of the temple buildings leak, and water has washed away parts of the paintings on the walls, or the plaster surface has crumbled away. Many of the old murals are too dim to be photographed. One craftsman works continually on the murals in the colonnade around Wat Phra Keo, the royal temple, trying to keep ahead of the deterioration. The government has covered some old murals with glass to protect them.

In former times, before people could read, murals were a form of instruction as well as decoration. Scenes from the lives of Buddha and worthy heroes might influence an observer to live a better life. Grim scenes of hell would warn a man of the punishments awaiting the evil; paintings of the many heavens would encourage him to be good. The murals had much the same purpose as those in the medieval churches of Europe, where paintings of the Madonna, of the life of Christ, and of the saints carried a message to the illiterate.

The earliest Thai murals were engraved on stone. Some have been found set in the walls of a ruined temple at Sukhodaya. They date from the thirteenth century and are Indian in style. They were probably inspired by drawings brought by Ceylonese monks who came to Sukhodaya to teach Buddhist doctrine. The oblong stones are incised with pictures in line and show episodes from the lives of Buddha before he attained full enlightenment. He was known then as *bodisattva*, or potential Buddha. One scene shows him in early life, when he was a dog. He sits on a conventionalized cushion, expounding doctrine to some kings, who listen with their hands folded together respectfully. In another he is shown in his life as a rich man, and he points at a wine jar and warns a group of four men to avoid alcohol. They look as though they had already had some of the contents of the jar!

Most of the murals painted at Sukhodaya have vanished with the years. A few fragments, painted towards the end of the thirteenth century, remain. They are done in pale vermillion monochrome with flowing outlines. They are in the style of the sculpture of the period but are not as fine artistically. Buddha is shown sitting between rows of worshiping figures. Sometimes he is in a painted, ornamental niche. The figures are in horizontal bands, one band above another, separated by strips of design.

No more murals have been found from this period. Some damaged murals made in the fifteenth century at the time of Ayudhya were discovered in the ruins of the city and in temple buildings in other places. For more than half a century the murals were still painted in the conventional design of figures in horizontal bands, but with the addition of decorative foliage, leaves of the bo tree, and simplified, painted architectural details. Until modern times all the colors used were harmonious, natural pigments made of earth and minerals. Yellow, black, and vermillion were used in these murals.

During the seventeenth and eighteenth centuries, after the fall of Ayudhya many new temples were being built in the new capital of Bangkok. Murals were painted in polychrome. Gold was added, especially on the jewelry worn by figures, and in architectural forms. These murals were more pictorial than formerly.

The artist did not try to show things literally. There are no shadows, the colors are flat, and the spaces are enclosed within a flowing outline. The story is painted in scenes

along a wall — episodes starting at the bottom of the composition, the events one above another. The scenes are
separated by borders of delicate design. In later periods
they were divided by trees, bushes, rocks, or a wall.

In a mural, Buddha stands or sits preaching, sometimes
with groups of disciples. He is in the positions used in images and old stone carvings. Painted niches about him
look very much like the stone niches on walls where a
statue was placed, and derive from them. Sometimes a
statue of Buddha stands before a scene on a painted wall,
and the statue is understood to be within the scene. Buddha is often depicted in the traditional position of over-
coming Mara, the evil one.

Murals illustrate events from the life of Buddha, or are
taken from the story "The Three Worlds," about heaven,
earth, and hell. At the top of the wall there may be paintings of fantastic, heavenly lands inhabited by supernatural
beings. Kinaras, half bird and half woman, float about
gracefully among celestial animals and plants. Below is the
earth, with its palaces and rulers. Lower still is hell, its
tormented inmates turning to a disciple of Buddha, who
has come to preach to them while they plead to be relieved
from their situation.

There are scenes from Thai fables and stories from the
Ramakien, the Thai version of the Indian epic called the
Ramayana, with its celestial beings, heroes, and animals.
The superior beings, kings, and princesses wear the same
crowns and garments that have been handed down from
the past and are found in the classical drama. Their traditional gestures express their emotions although their faces
remain expressionless. It is the same in the Thai theater.

Painted buildings with many roofs and pavilions rise one
above another. One seems to wander through a magic, toy-

like town as the story unwinds. There is the pleasure of
looking into secret gardens and over walls into the lives of
the painted characters. Everything is more, and also less,
than natural and takes on a sharp significance. Crowned
figures wearing triangular halos peer calmly at you through
open balconies or sit in the many-roofed houses. Above
the top-level walls and trees, clouds with curly edges float,
carrying along a goddess with her arms gracefully curved.

A long procession winds through a landscape of pre-
cisely drawn conventional rocks and bushes. The king
rides an elephant, preceded by retainers carrying many-
storied umbrellas suitable to his rank and fans such as one

*This temple wall mural is from a decadent period of
Thai art when perspective and shading was attempted.*

still sees in temples today. A rider hurries his horse so that
it can keep up with the elephant.

The artist shows more individuality and realism when
he depicts the common people, and often adds humor to
the more formal pictures. These scenes usually appear at
the edges or beneath the main subject, almost an after-
thought catering to the artist's whim. People go about
their daily occupations. Market women carry baskets, or
crowded together they prepare food outside a palace. An
old man sleeps; a young man tries to catch the attention
of a girl. The fighting dogs frighten a small boy, who over-
turns a basket of food while the onlookers try to hide their
smiles. These figures portray period costumes and life.

Until recently, artists were anonymous. There was no way
to reproduce a work of art except for an artist to copy it
according to his ability. Usually some of his own individuality appears in the copy. The artist was not trying for
originality, he was striving for superior workmanship. He
approached the work modestly and with appropriate ceremonies when he painted sacred subjects. He wished to
show that he did not presume to take part in religious
events.

The murals were painted in tempera on dry plaster,
which unfortunately does not last as well as frescoes
which are painted on walls while the plaster is wet. In dry
places tempera lasts well, but the climate of Thailand is
too humid. Some of the murals are only ghosts of their
former splendor.

When a wall was prepared for a mural, it was washed
many times. To remove any trace of salt, the water was
mixed with the pounded leaves of a special bush. Before
plaster was smoothed on, the wall was washed with clear

water. The plaster was made of chalk, bound with a paste of cooked tamarind seeds. When it became dry, the picture was drawn in outline with red ochre. Flat colors were applied with pigments made of earth and minerals mixed with a tree gum. Details were then added.

The brushes were made of bits of tree root cut flat, split, and set in silver handles. Others were made of bark that had been pounded at the end until it frayed. Fine lines were painted with a brush made of bullock hair.

A very thin mixture of the chalk and tamarind was also used on the cloth or paper on which a picture was to be painted. It did not hold very well, and the pictures had to be handled with care. These pictures are long hangings, over a yard wide and several yards long. They are covered with religious subjects in the same style as the murals. Temples owned sets of these hangings; monks displayed them on ceremonial days, and they could be taken from the temple for outside ceremonies.

The temple books, made of palm leaves, are kept in sets, wrapped in cloth, and stored in bookcases. These black-and-gold lacquer cases are the most beautiful form of Thai art. The cases are of several varieties. Some are shoulder height, narrowing slightly at the top, and thirty inches deep. They stand on short legs or on a pedestal. Two doors, hinged at the sides, make up the front panel. Inside there are shelves to hold the bundles of books.

Some books are kept in large chests originally used to hold the clothes of wealthy people. Often, when the owner died, his relatives would present the chest to the monastery.

A smaller, oblong box is about a yard long and fourteen inches high, with a lid that fits flat in the top. It holds the palm-leaf books that are read during ceremonies for the

dead. The books are on spiritual subjects concerning the future life, with its rewards and punishments.

When a monk goes outside the temple to preach, his attendant carries a small portable box, four inches high, four inches wide, and long enough to hold the length of a palm book. As the panels on this box are small, they are only decorated with designs. Conventionalized scenes and figures are used on the larger ones, with bars of pure design running along the strips that separate the panels, and forming the borders along the edges.

The best of the lacquer cases were made in the Ayudhya period in the seventeenth century. As they were kept in many temples throughout the country, they were not all destroyed during the Burmese attacks, and many beautiful specimens survive.

Their entire surface is covered with two-dimensional decoration. The artist must keep a perfect balance between the areas of black and gold; neither should predominate in the design. Large spaces are covered with varied and delicate detail, so that no part will stand out unduly. Fine linear patterns are used in the clothing of the figures, on parts of the surface of animals, and in the architectural features of the same delightful towns that are found in the murals. All seems to be turned to gold by a Midas.

The backgrounds are usually filled with conventionalized foliage, flowers, grasses, or trees inspired by the luxuriant growth of the tropics. This may be more or less

A battle scene from a gold leaf and black lacquer panel. On the right is the three-tiered umbrella.

geometrical or freely flowing, suggesting flames or swaying seaweed, in an upward, vertical movement. There are
vinelike scrolls, winding one above another, the ends forming mythological beings.

The backgrounds surround figures of kings, angels,
heroes, and demons. They wear crowns, headdresses, or
pointed, leaf-shaped halos. A small space of black is left
around the head, so that it may stand out from the background. There are fighting monkeys with masklike faces,
posing as actors do in the theater. Animals, although
stylized, show their own characteristics. All are full of
energy and vitality. Squirrels and other small animals may
peer from the foliage, and birds or butterflies seem to
flutter about. They are drawn more naturalistically than
the larger animals and reveal the artists' close observation
of nature.

One box panel shows Turapee, the son of the ruler of
the water buffaloes. He caused the death of his father, and
is being punished by Hanuman, the monkey king, who

attacks him. The surrounding foliage seems to swing with the combat as the monkey clings to a horn and a leg of the kicking animal. The buffalo's tail and horns curve with the lines of the stems of leaves in the background.

A hero may ride to combat in a curved chariot or on a striding elephant in full regalia. Smaller figures scatter about, full of action.

Two combatants, a monkey and a demon or two warriors, swords and clubs brandished high, show a dancing quality. They seem lively but not vicious. The figure placed in the higher position is considered the winner.

Much more skill is needed in the technique and designing of these lacquer objects than is necessary in mural painting. The wooden surfaces are covered with three coats of black lacquer made from resin. The lacquer is rubbed to a smooth surface, and the design, which has been previously drawn with the utmost care, is traced on it. All parts that are to remain black are painted over with a gummy yellow substance which is allowed to dry. The entire surface is then covered with a thin coat of lacquer. When this is partially dry, gold leaf is pressed all over the lacquer. The box is set aside for twenty hours and then it is washed with water. The water carries away the yellow paint along with the gold leaf that is above it, leaving the intricate black-and-gold design, with distinct lines and edges. Many of the lines are as thin as those in a pen drawing. The Thai name for this process means "ornament washed out with water" — an apt expression.

The gold-and-black-lacquer work is still used in many things, such as small boxes, trays, and bowls, but the modern work does not compare with the old in design and execution.

Window shutters and door panels in temples and palaces are covered with designs showing guardian spirits in gold-and-black lacquer. Even whole walls containing hundreds of square feet were once covered with designs and pictures.

The National Museum in Bangkok has a large collection of the old book containers. In some of the temples large book containers can still be seen standing along the walls. They appear at their best in such a beautiful setting. A faint light comes through the deep-set, narrow windows. Candles flicker before the altar, where a gigantic figure of Buddha sits on his gilded pedestal, the gold flame on his head hidden in the dimness. Under the high roof the incense wreathes about in faint spirals.

The roof is supported by large columns. Each column is carefully painted with a repeating pattern, rising from bands of design at the base. All is as evenly drawn as the pattern on wallpaper. The murals on the pictured walls are mysterious. Probably no one knows how their story ends for the upper part is lost in the shadows.

Bare feet pad across the marble paving, as a few worshipers come to sit solemnly on the floor. A monk, seated on a carved bench, reads quietly in Pali, the language of sacred writings. The Buddha smiles over their heads. The air is cool inside after the burning sun. A breeze stirs the tiny silver bells that hang from the outside eaves. Their tinkling, faintly heard over the monk's intoning, sounds like singing insects.

Though many of the people do not understand the words as they are spoken in Pali, they enjoy the peace and beauty, and the pictured walls help to carry a religious message to them.

9

Those That Lurk in the Shadows

*"A coward that fears ghosts does not travel far,
a brave man goes a long way."*

Long before the teachings of Buddha came to Thailand,
people worshiped local gods and nature spirits. Many
mountain tribes still do. Spirits were thought to be everywhere, controlling most of the conditions of life and the
vagaries of nature. Many of the old beliefs are dying out,
thanks to Buddhism, but supernatural beings and ghosts
still lurk in the imagination of the less educated.

There are hundreds of types of spirits in Thailand.
Those that are evil must be placated; the more kindly ones
must be persuaded to give their help. It is safer not to
neglect them. They are all called *phi* — celestial beings,
ghosts, and elemental nature spirits.

The phi of the heavens, having reached the heights
through meritorious living, never bother human beings. A
shooting star is not sinister; it is only a celestial dweller
dropping to earth to take on mortal form in order to atone
for some fault committed.

Many other essentially benevolent spirits may be easily
provoked by discourtesy or neglect.

Some phi are mischievous and wish to be frightening.
They may cause a sudden darkness, or pinch a person

unexpectedly. Like the will-o'-the-wisp, a phi can mislead a traveler. A light flickers across a field. A man, thinking it is shining in his own house, quickens his step as he hurries towards home. Suddenly he stumbles into a muddy bog, or tears his clothes in a thorny tangle of vines that clutch and hold him.

Spirits can be very malevolent and take many forms. They haunt old ruins and houses, and are apt to lurk in lonely places or dark roads at night. Certain phantoms cause frightful diseases to anyone who sleeps in their haunts; or in the form of a black goblin-monkey they may suck the blood of a wayfarer in the forest.

Another bloodsucker is a horrible phi one hundred feet tall. It is the ghost of some wicked person. It is emaciated. Its mouth is so tiny that it is difficult for it to eat and its hunger is never satisfied. It makes a weird, thin whistling as it breathes. When a person hears this sound, it may be too late for him to escape. When the phi comes across a sleeping person, it greedily sucks his blood, leaving small red marks on the skin as though dozens of mosquitoes had been busy during the night.

The jungle is particularly fearsome and full of all kinds of phi. Within the deep forest it is easy to believe in spirits — even in the daytime. Light flickers back and forth through heavy foliage; shadows come and go. Something half-seen seems to be moving; then, as a man turns fearfully to look, it is gone. All is quiet, then suddenly a puff of breeze rustles the treetops, whispering softly. A hidden strand of vine tugs at one's feet, a clawlike hand. Tales are told of men who went into the forest and were transformed into sinister shapes, or were never seen again.

In the last century, nearly everyone wore charms to ward off evil, and many people still do so today. They believe

that an amulet hung on a chain around the neck will protect them. The amulet is usually a small statue of Buddha
or a plaque with a Buddhist symbol made of silver or clay.
Sometimes the amulet is engraved with cabalistic signs or
words and rolled to form a cylinder; sometimes a paper
with words written on it is enclosed in the tube. Mostly
the young people wear these, as the elderly rely more on
the Buddhist religion and the making of merit.

It is a good idea to provide a home for the spirit that
haunts a special site. Small houses are built for it near
roads. Where a tree has been cut down, a new home for
the phi that used to dwell in the tree must be provided.

When land is cleared for a new dwelling, one of these
small houses is erected on the site, for the tutelary spirit
called *Phra Phum*, which means "lord of the land." He is
the former occupant of the property. If treated well, this
phi becomes the protector of the family and of the house
where they live, but he might make mischief if neglected.
He is somewhat like Puck in English legends. On an
auspicious day, the spot for the spirit's house is selected
with care. The shadow of the main dwelling must never
fall across that of the Phra Phum. The worlds of men and
spirits should not mingle. On a waterway, where houses
are very close together, the spirit house is put on a stake in
the water in order to avoid the shadows.

When a hole has been dug to hold the post for the Phra
Phum's house, an offering of red and white rice cakes is
placed before it. Candles and incense are lighted. Then
the post and house are erected, sprinkled with lustral
water, and the Phra Phum invited to enter his new abode.

The Phra Phum likes frequent offerings, and he is always remembered on special occasions and holydays. In
return he will keep away bad spirits and general misfor-

tune. Sometimes, when something especially unlucky has occurred, he is promised very fine gifts if he will help. Would he like an elephant, some servants, a buffalo, or even a motorcar? When the gifts are presented they are only tokens of the real thing, figures made of clay by the offerer, or bought in the local market.

When visitors arrive to stay overnight, they must give the family phi an offering and ask permission to stay and be under his protection. In some parts of Thailand the Phra Phum objects to visitors who stay over three days — a convenience for hosts.

People often make the wood and thatch houses for the Phra Phum themselves. So many houses are needed for

various phi that there are also workshops that make them. A regular city of small houses stands in the yard before the work shed — something for every taste. They have steep, overlapping roofs like those seen in temples, and the same type of gable ends, elaborate or simplified. Sometimes four sets of roofs meet in the form of a cross, with a finial where they join together.

The roof is supported on fancy columns above a platform. The sides are open — all except for a room at the back, which has side walls for the spirit's comfort. Offerings are placed on this platform.

Some of the houses are made of rough, unfinished wood. The roof tiles are represented by strips of scalloped wood set one above the other. They cost so little that anyone can afford one. Some houses are painted with bright colors, or a lucky phi may have an elaborate dwelling made of many-hued stucco.

In very small towns there may be no individual spirit houses but one shrine for the whole community. Each town once had a guardian spirit, possibly that of a general who died long ago defending the place and who still takes an interest in it. Or it may be the spirit of the land.

At Bangkok a shrine was dedicated to the guardian spirit a long time ago. It still stands, a small square building surmounted by a spire. A carved wooden column stands inside. This contains the spirit. About it in the dim light are lesser phi. The house is cluttered with offerings given by the superstitious who have asked a favor. Old candle wax sticks up in grimy blobs. The air smells of dust, stale incense, and dried-up flowers. Small squares of gold are smeared in layers upon the post. Clay votive gifts lie about, covered with a soft coating of dust like mole fur. Paper prayers are stuck one above another, some new, the

paper of others peeling, shredded, and brown, put there
generations ago for old, forgotten boons.

When someone is ill, and it is difficult to reach one of the
many doctors trained in modern medicine, a spirit doctor
might be called in. There are not enough trained doctors
for every small village or peasant community to have one.
A local person who claims to be able to cure diseases is
likely to be called upon for help. He may have read a few
ancient medical books that are kept at the wat, or he may
be a spirit doctor who believes in magic. These doctors are
not blamed if the patient does not recover; instead it is believed that the spirit that caused the illness was too strong.

The spirit may be evil or it may be a spirit offended in
some way. Rites must be used to exorcise it. Offerings and
promises of gifts are made to the family Phra Phum. Relatives may beat on the floor of their house with sticks to
drive the evil spirit away.

When the spirit doctor arrives, he chants spells. He may
sprinkle the patient with especially prepared water. He
inquires where any pains are felt. Then he takes a mud
figure that he has prepared with incantations, gives it the
name of the patient, and pricks it in the places where the
patient suffers. The spirit thinks the mud figure is the patient and may be driven forth. Sometimes the mud doll is
put on a tray with some object that has belonged to the
sick person. Food is there for the spirit to eat. While the
spirit doctor chants spells, the spirit is tempted by the
food, and after it has eaten, it enters the clay figure by
mistake. Some brave member of the family carries the tray
to a crossroads, and hastily runs home. When the spirit has
recovered from the hearty meal, it is too late for it to find
its way back to the house of the patient.

It is in the interest of the local sorcerer to encourage superstition and to induce people to believe in his powers so they will pay him money for performing his rites and for the amulets he sells.

The sorcerer tells an awed client of the dangers involved in obtaining a magic ingredient for curing an illness. He tells how he went out at night, after the moon had set, to a place haunted by such a terrible ghost that it was avoided by the villagers even in the daytime. He sat there watching, by the flame of a small candle, until he heard the eerie hooting of an owl. He knew the Lord of Death and Darkness rode by on its back. Then he started incantations to conjure the unearthly one for help. Endlessly chanting spells, he leaned slowly forward and held his candle beneath the chin of the ghastly ghost who appeared. The sorcerer's shadow weaved about, but the ghost had none. Soon the heat of the candle caused fat and oil to drop sizzling from the ghost's chin, and the sorcerer caught them in a shallow, earthenware dish.

Anyone can understand what potent and dangerous material this is, and what a powerful charm it becomes when correctly mixed with secret ingredients! And how wise and brave is the sorcerer!

Much higher in rank than the sorcerers are the astrologers. They were once very important personages in Thailand. Individual astrologers held honored positions in court. They watched the heavens for signs and omens, and pored over books of magic and charts. The king consulted them to determine the auspicious day for his personal matters and before planning affairs of state. The astrologers foretold the correct time for state ceremonies, a king's coronation, or a royal cremation. They decided on which day a new temple or palace should be started and when the king should take a journey or begin a war — no doubt allowing plenty of time for preparation.

The court astrologer was held responsible for the outcome of these affairs. When his predictions were correct, he was honored and showered with gifts. When they were wrong, he was degraded, or even beaten. His must have been a difficult job!

The astrologer today is far removed from his former high estate. Some individuals, however, still consult one to find out the auspicious day for special undertakings.

A person's horoscope depends in part on the year in which he was born. The years are arranged in a cycle of twelve, each dedicated to a different animal. The cycle starts with the rat, then rotates to the ox, the tiger, the hare, the dragon, the snake, the horse, the goat, the monkey, the cock, the dog, and the pig. The animals of the Thai year are often depicted in Thai art.

A Thai must treat the animal of his year with special kindness for it is under his protection. How difficult it must be to cherish the rat or the snake!

Astrologers, soothsayers, and spirits are not recognized officially by the Buddhist religion, and it discourages people from depending on them. But even devout Buddhists sometimes take part in spirit rites, believing, partly, because such things have always been done. It can do no actual harm — they rationalize — and it is well to be safe.

It may not be long before most of the Thai are no more superstitious than the many Westerners who vaguely think it better not to pass beneath a ladder or begin anything important on Friday the thirteenth.

10

The Thai Speak and Write

*"The sweetness of palm sugar shall pass,
but the sweetness of words lives on."*

The Thai language is uninflected and contains no preposi-
tions or conjunctions. Verbs do not change their tense.
The plural of nouns is formed by a phrase; for instance,
"three oranges" becomes "orange three round things," or
"three horses," "horse three bodies." The qualifying word
varies with each type of object. Sentences are arranged in
the order of subject-verb-object. Each word may be followed by a word to qualify it. When a Thai says that a
big, black buffalo is chasing two small boys, its form is
literally "Buffalo black body big chase boy two persons
small."

When the Thai came in contact with the Khmer of
Cambodia, whose culture derived from India, they adopted
words of Pali and Sanskrit origin. These words were poly-
syllabic and were chiefly used for abstract ideas, literature,
and upper-class speech. The speech of the educated classes
became a very different thing from that of the peasants.
Sanskrit and Pali were used for communication between
countries of Indian and Buddhist culture, in much the
same way as Latin was used in Europe as the language of
diplomacy.

When contact was made with the West, many European words were adopted and often shortened to suit the Thai tongue. They were needed to express new ideas and things that were being introduced into the country even though the Thai were ingenious in combining their old words to describe innovations. Two or more words formed a new idea. A train became "carriage fire," and a match was called "stick rub fire." This was a continuation of a habit of combining words to express another idea. "Fruit," for instance, is " child of the tree," a bullet is "child of the gun," honey is "water of bees." The word for heart is combined with other words to express emotion. "Obstructed heart" means "angry." "Unbursting heart" means "relieved." As with us, a "good heart" means "kindly."

Different words are used for the same thing depending upon the person addressed — an inferior, an equal, or a superior. "You" and "I" vary in these situations. More and more syllables are added as deference increases. To a noble, a man says "I, the servant of the lord." To a prince he says "I, the servant of the excellent." To the King he must say "I, the servant under excellent feet."

Many Thai phrases are poetical in expression. It is not polite to say a direct "no," so other forms are used: "I have considered, and do not find it so," or "It is not in accordance with my heart." In ordinary family talk, "vacant" or "empty" are the words for "no," and are often accompanied by a waving of a hand from side to side in front of the body, palm outwards.

The Thai delight in choosing words that sound pleasant together, and admire alliteration and good rhythm in speech. Humorous sentences are composed of a few words repeated in various meanings. They use poetic similes, and express humor in plays on words. Even in everyday speech they have many words that have imagination and symbolism. A tiger's tail is called his "rudder," a shoe is a "foot-boat," and whisky is "sin water." The horizon is "feet of the sky." Knots in a tree are called its "eyes."

There are many traditional proverbs and folk sayings. They contain shrewd wisdom in a terse phrase with a double meaning. A proverb often has more of the characteristics of a people than its formal writing, for it has developed naturally and is not a conscious art. These folk sayings are difficult to translate without losing some of the flavor and punning humor. They may be in prose or in two lines of doggerel rhyme, each line with a separate sense as well as a meaning as a whole. Some of the sayings have much the same meaning as a corresponding proverb in English. "Don't buy a buffalo in a pool" means much the same as "Don't buy a pig in a poke."

"When clearing rattan, do not leave the sprouts," means do not do a half-way job, or do not leave something to return to plague you. "The pole does not always reach the water," refers to an inadequate person.

Every Thai seems to have a natural aptitude for impromptu verse, and rhyming contests are popular. After the rice is harvested and the workers have put in a long day threshing the grain from the sheaves, they relax together under the starry sky in the evening, squatting around a small fire on the threshing ground.

The smoke helps to keep mosquitoes away as it drifts about in the light breeze. The firelight glints on the happy faces in the circle and the surrounding background of discarded rice straw. Sometimes twelve men and women will stand in a ring, each with a sheaf in one hand, a sickle in the other. Feet are stamped to mark time. Sheaves and sickles are swung in imitation of reaping, as the circle moves round. One of the men sings a "bird call." One of the women answers a "response," accepting the challenge, and the contest is on. The challenger starts a rhyme about any subject — perhaps a lofty idea, or more likely something that has happened during the day, perhaps village gossip. The woman across the circle takes it up. Each tries to give the most exaggerated mock compliment or mock insult, or the most unanswerable retort. The main rule of the game is that each line must end with the same rhyme sound or assonance, and the contest ends when one side or the other runs out of rhymes. Between the lines the rest of the chorus of workers chant a chorus of nonsense, rather like the Elizabethan "Hey-nonny-nonny." Rhymesters are so much valued on these occasions that sometimes a skilled one receives two days' labor on his own farm in exchange for one day's labor on his neighbor's.

A flirtatious exchange might go somewhat like this (the chorus of nonsense that would actually follow each line of the exchange is omitted):

(He starts) *"My friends all came and warned me, you were flighty as a bird."*

(She answers) *"And when you came a-courting me, your song could not be heard."*

(He appeals to the spectators) *"Her yard was full of bullfrogs, so she could not hear a word."*

(She sings disgustedly) *"For song and croak were just alike — the likeness was absurd."* And so on.

Until recently, colloquial Thai was not used in literature. The literature was written in the more formal language, but it shows the same pleasure in poetic thought and rhythmic sentences.

The earliest writing in Thailand is on stone steles. These have been found all over Thailand, some dating back to the sixth century. It was a meritorious act to set up the steles where a passer-by could see them and be instructed. Some recorded the names of kings, some the deeds of holy people or sayings of Buddha. The writing on the early ones is in Sanskrit or Pali. The first known use of the Thai language and alphabet is on a stele dated 1292 A.D. It is a large stone, domed at the top, and incised with even, beautifully spaced letters. It was designed by King Rama Khamhaeng, who reigned in the kingdom of Sukhodaya. The king devised a variation of the Khmer, or Cambodian script suited to the Thai language.

The modern Thai alphabet contains fifty-eight characters. A mark is placed above a syllable to indicate the tone in which it should be spoken. Another diacritical mark indicates that a syllable should not be pronounced, for long Pali words, when adopted into Thai, are shortened in speaking. Writing is decorative, flowing from left to right, without spaces between the words of a paragraph.

The earliest manuscripts that have been preserved are religious works. One contains rules of conduct for the monastic orders, another an early conception of the universe, with a description of the endless cycles of life. There is a Thai version of the life of Buddha, with hundreds of the legends that have grown up around the original story.

"It is not in accordance with my heart"

ยังไม่ถูกใจฉัน   TYPEWRITTEN

ยังไม่ถูกใจฉัน   HANDWRITTEN

For many centuries, religious works were written on pages made from the side leaves cut from the stiff midrib of palm fronds. They are still used for religious books. The pages were tied in bundles and placed between narrow boards, then trimmed to the correct size with a semicircular knife. After pressing, the leaves were sanded until the surface was smooth. Then words were incised with a stylus — a sharp point set in a fat, cigar-shaped handle. Ink made of soot and wood oil was rubbed across the incised surface and then wiped off, and the leaf was again scoured with sand. The ink remained in the incisions and the background was clean. Both sides of the page were used and the edges were sometimes painted red or gilded.

The sheets, about two and a half inches wide and eighteen inches long, were bound with silk cords through holes punched in the ends. The books had covers of silver or carved ivory, or were set with patterns in pearl shell. The leaves were often illuminated with decorative designs.

New books were copied from older ones by hand, sometimes by monks. As a meritorious act, the words might be copied laboriously and exactly by pious people or by court ladies who could not even read.

Later books were made of paper. A sheet many yards long and about a foot wide was folded back and forth in pleats, forming pages which were not cut apart. The earliest one extant dates from the sixteenth century. This type of book was still made in the nineteenth century. The paper was made of tree bark beaten to a pulp. It was soaked in water and poured in a thin layer into a shallow box. The bottom of the box was a strainer covered by thin cloth, so the water could drain out. The pulp, dried in the sun, became a soft paper.

The paper for books was either left white or blackened. The writing on white paper was done with a bamboo splinter dipped in black ink. Gamboge, a tree gum, was made into yellow ink and used on black paper, or the writing was done with crayons made of crushed gamboge or white chalk.

For people who sit on the floor, the folding manuscript book was convenient. It could be spread out with many folds showing at one time. The illustrations often used more space than the writing; some stories were told without text.

The subjects treated in these books are not necessarily religious. There are books on philosophy, architecture, and military tactics. Some tell the rules for astrology, or for alchemy, with designs of mystic formulas, and pictures showing how to arrange articles used in magic rites. A medical book is illustrated with drawings of human figures, with areas indicated for massage, and with pictures showing how to cure various diseases. Another gives yoga-like exercises for hermits. The hermit is dressed only in a cloth

This ink-on-paper rubbing is from a temple ruins at Angkor Vat thought to be seven to eight centuries old.

around his middle and he wears a crown. A mythical beast stares at him from some bits of foliage.

There are treatises on trees, birds, and the care of pets written in verse and with delightful drawings. A book with faded red folds tells the rules for theatrical performances; the figures are painted in gold and colors, the designs balanced by sprays of foliage.

There are rules for functions and ceremonies at the palace, and codes of laws. Many laws that are five hundred years old are still in use.

Many religious books and some on other subjects were kept in monasteries all over Thailand, and so were preserved when the library at Ayudhya was burned during the sack of the city by the Burmese. So many historical records and chronicles were lost that much of old history has had to be reconstructed from fragmentary writings and from the annals of other countries. There are records in Burma of their wars. A king of Ayudhya, who was captured by the Burmese, was asked about his country and told long tales of past history which a Burmese scribe took down. Portuguese and French travelers have also left records.

The Thai call history "the biography of kings." Royalty wrote much of it. They were the only ones who could record the acts of their predecessors with truth, as they did not need to use the praise and flattery that respect would demand from a lesser writer.

Literature was the most respected of the arts and was entirely the product of the upper classes. Authors were educated at court under the patronage of the king and nobles, who often wrote themselves or collaborated with a corps of writers. A king was often given credit for writing works done during his reign.

King Narai was one of Thailand's most illustrious kings. During his reign art flourished. One of the writers under Narai's patronage, unfortunately anonymous, is famed for his dramas and graceful verse. As a child, he was sent to the court to be educated, and wrote some plays in which his playmates acted. They may not have been skilled actors, but the plays were so good that the king noticed their merit. He had the boy instructed in writing, and in the literary classics of India and Persia. (Much of Thai literature was derived from these countries.) When the boy grew up, his works showed originality, power, and beauty, and they have become Thai classics.

King Narai enjoyed having the classics read to him. A French ambassador who came to Ayudhya in 1685 wrote that the king took a nap after his chief meal, reposing on an embroidered mat. Nearby a reader, who practically lay on the floor with respect, held a book on the ground before him. He started reading in a loud voice, gradually lowering it more and more until the king's eyes closed and his

*Skanda, god of war, is depicted in this rubbing from
one of the temples at the famed ruins at Angkor Vat.*

breathing became heavy. Then the reader crawled away, to return in due time, starting to read again in such a loud voice that the king was forced to awake. Thus no one rudely awakened him.

The old Thai works are almost all written in poetry, as are the early tales in most countries. Before there were many books, people would gather in the market places to hear stories recited by a minstrel. It was easier for him to remember the tales in rhyme than in prose. The minstrels kept time with wooden castanets as they intoned their stories, and at intervals they sang. They often made up episodes to add to the old tales.

Thai poetry uses rhyme, assonance, and alliteration, with patterns based on the tones of words. There are different types of poetry for religious subjects, dramatic poems, and short lyrics.

Some long tales in poetry tell of imaginary journeys, mostly a theme on which to hang romantic verses about a lady's beauty. Things seen while traveling remind the poet of her and the sadness he feels because of her absence. Some of the connecting verses contain information about the customs and ways of living at the time they were written. Love songs taken from these poems are sung by the Thai today.

Many fine poems have been written about Queen Suriyothai, one of the greatest historical heroines of Thailand. During the Thai wars with the Burmese she dressed as a warrior and, riding an elephant, accompanied her husband to battle. During the fighting, a Burmese leader challenged the king to a duel. The two leaders crashed their elephants together, slashing at each other furiously with long, curved swords. Queen Suriyothai saw that her husband was losing and in danger of his life. She forced her elephant between the two contestants, received the deadly blow intended for the king, and was killed. Her husband had time to recover, and won the duel.

Many dramatic stories were adapted from old myths of India, as in the *Ramakien*, the Thai version of the epic *Ramayana*. It became Thai in feeling and details, with many interpolated stories and touches of Thai humor. The stories were no longer religious, but were intended for entertainment. King Rama I, who reigned from 1782, wrote and edited a version of the *Ramakien* that filled many volumes. He included accounts of Thai royal traditions and of state ceremonies and functions. Many Thai writers and poets have used episodes from the *Ramakien* for their works, and stories from it are used in the Thai classical dance drama.

Since 1850 most Thai literature has been in prose. Letters and proclamations by King Mongkut (1851-1868), and by his son King Chulalongkorn, are written in such a fine style that they influenced later Thai writings. King Mongkut's personal letters to his family are charming, sincere, and affectionate. They are full of well-described details.

Old classics were rewritten many times and adapted for readers of different periods, using contemporary backgrounds and characters. Soon Thai authors started writing popular novels. These books were no longer only for the upper classes. As more people were learning to read, the writers began to use lower-class situations. The influence of Western literature led to serious fiction dealing with economic problems in a realistic way, and many works of nonfiction have been written. The King today offers a prize for the most original work written by a Thai.

The National Library at Bangkok has the best collection

of foreign books in the Orient. There are old Thai books and old manuscripts written in Pali, Sanskrit, and Chinese. Stone steles with ancient inscriptions are kept at the library. There is a reading room for the public which contains newspapers and magazines in many languages. The library also publishes books. Today, most of the people in Thailand can read and can own books.

11

Thai Tales and Fables

"Many strands make up a rope."

When the minstrels wandered about Thailand, they told tales to the countrypeople who could not read. These tales grew into a wealth of stories apart from the classics of Thai literature. Like the folk sayings, they contained simple humor and advice: how one man tried to get the best of another — sometimes by using ruses or disguises — or turned a small possession into great wealth. Such cunning is admired; a man should be alert to conquer any difficulties that befall him. No sympathy is given to a man as stupid as a buffalo.

Animals represent certain characteristics — as they do with us. As well as the buffalo, which is stupid and ignorant, there is the crocodile, which represents duplicity and ferocity; the deer, which is gentle and meek like our lamb; the myna bird, which is talkative and repetitive like our parrot; and many others.

There is often a proverb attached to a tale as a warning. The following fable shows that too great greed makes fortune leave.

The wife and children of a hunter were hungry, and there was no food in the house. So the hunter took his bow to the forest, where he saw an elephant, and wounded it with a poisoned arrow. The pain caused the elephant to pursue the hunter, in order to kill him.

The fleeing hunter reached a tall ant heap. He scrambled to the top without noticing a poisonous snake that lay there in the sun. Angered, the snake struck the hunter with its fangs. The man retaliated by killing the snake. Then he died, still holding his drawn bow. When the pursuing elephant arrived, it too, fell dead from the poisoned arrow in its side.

A hungry wolf came past. "Hah!" it cried, "here is enough to feed me for a long time."

As it approached, slavering, it thought, "Why waste the leather bowstring? It will be a good start for my meal." The wolf bit the cord in two. When it broke, the bow sprung and one end hit the wolf on the head. The wolf died at once.

In longer, romantic tales, mortals mix with supernatural beings. Girls with wings fly from the sky to earth. Sometimes one is captured or falls in love with a mortal. Difficult feats are demanded of heroes, and magicians may give them aid. A fierce crocodile may change into human form to abduct the daughter of a noble, only finally to be overcome by a mortal. There is a sad tale of a lady imprisoned and guarded by a magic spear. When the lady's lover tries to rescue her, the spear stabs him to death.

The story of the *Jealous Ricebird* contains birds that are reborn as humans. A romance, a princess and a commoner, magic and clever trickery — enough for any tale!

Once two ricebirds built their nest in a bamboo thicket at the edge of the rice fields. The wife stayed at home to look after their only nestling and the husband went out to look for food. He flew across the new, green rice to a lotus pond and saw a pink lotus flower raising its head above the water. He jumped upon it and started to eat the delicious seeds inside the flower. He ate and he ate and did not notice the lengthening shadows. As the sun set, the petals of the lotus closed over him. The bird struggled hard, but could not free himself. He was shut in the flower for the night, so he settled down and went to sleep.

When morning came and the sun rose, the lotus gradually opened again. Carrying some seed with him, the bird flew as quickly as he could to his nest.

To his horror there was no nest and no baby's hungry open mouth. There were only embers and ashes where the bamboo clump had stood, and his wife was lamenting nearby.

"Wife, what has happened?" he cried.

She turned away from him. "How dare you speak to me, you rascal!" she cried. "You were away all of last night and I could not save our child from the fire." She sobbed harder than ever.

"Has our dear child died in this terrible fire?" said the husband with a gasp.

"Go away, you wicked bird!" the wife cried. "You were away when I needed you. I tried and tried but could not carry the baby alone. Now you come back when it is too late, you heartless thing."

"My wife, I could not come home," answered the husband sadly. "I was getting food and did not notice the time. I was trapped in a lotus, and could not get away. Please understand."

"Understand!" she shrilled. "Lotus, indeed! I can smell scented lotion on you, you must have been at a party all night, you faithless creature." She sobbed as loudly as ever.

The husband sighed. "Oh, that cursed lotus! Please listen to me —"

But the wife interrupted angrily. "No! I do not want to hear any more. Go out of my sight forever!" Between sobs she prayed. "Oh! Highest Power, if I must be born into this world again, please make me hate all men. I have had enough of them this time." Then she fell over and died of a broken heart.

The little husband, overcome with grief, also prayed. "Let me follow her wherever she may be and give me time to explain and again to be her husband."

He wandered about sadly with his unhappy memories until he, too, died of sorrow.

In her next life, the female ricebird was reborn as a beautiful princess, the only daughter of a king. According to her wish, she never liked nor talked to any man, although she had a kind and sweet nature.

The King was unhappy about her and sent messengers throughout his kingdom saying that any man who could make his daughter talk to him should have her hand in marriage.

A handsome young man named Sanpasit, who had been the male ricebird before his rebirth, heard the King's announcement. He had learned some magic, and one of the things he could do was send the spirit of one thing into another. So he asked his best friend to help him try his luck with the princess. The King was not very hopeful when they came to his palace, as many had tried and failed, but he had them conducted to the room of the Princess.

As they stood before the carved door, Sanpasit explained to his friend what he wished him to do. "Lend me your spirit for a while, when I am with the Princess." The

friend sat on the steps outside the door, and Sanpasit murmured a few spells.

When Sanpasit entered the room, the Princess would
not look at him. With his magic power, he put the spirit
of his friend in several places and talked to him on many
subjects, hoping the Princess would join in the conversa-
tion, but she looked at the floor and said nothing. At last

he put the spirit in a gold box beside the Princess.

"Fine box," said Sanpasit, "I would like to make friends with you. I am sure you could tell me some interesting things."

A small voice answered, seeming to come from a large ruby in the lid of the box. "How could I" it said. "I have been here for years and never seen the outside world. It is you who could tell me things of interest — please be kind and do so."

"All right," said Sanpasit, "I will tell you a story." The Princess glanced at him with interest, then quickly turned her face away again.

"There were once four friends," Sanpasit began. "One was a fortuneteller and could foretell the future, one was a famous marksman, one a skillful diver, and the fourth could restore life.

"They were walking by the bank of a river one day, when suddenly the teller of fortunes exclaimed, 'A big eagle is carrying a beautiful girl this way and will be here in a minute.'

"The men watched and soon the giant bird appeared overhead.

"At once the marksman aimed at it and his arrow killed the eagle at the first shot. The bird fell to the bottom of the river with the girl. The diver jumped into the water and brought her to the surface, but she was dead. Then the life restorer called the girl back to life.

"Now, box," asked Sanpasit, "which one of the four deserved to win the beautiful girl in marriage?"

The box replied, "The life restorer, of course, as he was the one who brought the girl back to life."

The princess could keep quiet no longer. She burst out, "No! What nonsense! How could the life restorer bring her back to life if she remained at the bottom of the river? The diver should be the winner. He was the only one who could dive in such deep water."

The king and queen, who were hidden outside the door, exclaimed with joy at the sound of her voice. "She talks! She talks!"

Sanpasit stood up and went from the room. He took the spirit of his friend with him and restored it to its owner. The friend awoke at once.

The king went to his daughter. "You spoke to Sanpasit," he said. "Do you like him, my child?"

"I do not hate him," answered the princess, "but I did not talk to him."

"But who else could you have been speaking with, daughter?" asked the king.

"Only with my gold box here," said the princess.

The king shook his head. "How could that be? Show me then how it talks."

The princess tried to make the box speak but it said nothing, so the King said, "My dear, do not be afraid; if you like Sanpasit, marry him. I have given my word and will do everything I can to make you happy."

The princess was half-reluctant, but she agreed.

The king gave them a magnificent wedding, with hundreds of elephants dressed in their best. Many-tiered umbrellas and ceremonial fans were carried in the procession, and the whole court was there in splendid costumes.

The princess overcame her objection to men and loved the handsome Sanpasit so they lived happily together, and the two ricebirds had a chance to make a new start.

12

The Thai Make Music

"Any man may add dew to the sea."

In the old days kings and princes kept troupes of musicians in their palaces, who were always ready to entertain their patron and his guests. There was friendly rivalry between the troupes, and the competition kept up a high standard of performance and led to the creation of much new music.

When, in 1932, a more democratic government replaced the old form of monarchy, Western influences altered the old way of life and traditional music almost ceased to exist. There was one period when the premier forbade the use of Thai instruments in an attempt to make Thailand more Western. Fortunately this ban did not last. The Department of Fine Arts and a few private schools in Bangkok today are trying to reinstate and preserve the old traditional music and dance by giving a series of concerts and performances every year, and sponsoring a school where they are taught. Members of the department are also collecting and preserving traditional music by using a system of notation based on our Western staff and notes. Music is also being recorded on tape. The radio and television stations give some time to the playing of traditional music.

A traditional ensemble of musicians is made up of from

five to twenty players who sit on the floor with their instruments. The Department of Fine Arts has listed more than fifty types of musical instruments, but some of these are only found in certain parts of the country; others which are shown in old illustrated manuscripts, are no longer in use today.

Instruments are classified into four groups: percussion instruments that play melodies, percussion instruments that play rhythm, wind instruments, and stringed instruments.

The main melody in an ensemble is played on a melodic percussion instrument, called Gong Wong Yai, which consists of a set of fifteen small gongs placed in order horizontally around an almost circular, low frame of cane. The player sits in the center of the circle and plays on the tops of the gongs with two mallets, one in each hand. This mallet is a stick with a hard, round piece of leather attached to the end. The melody is sometimes played in single notes and sometimes in octaves or fourths. This is the first instrument that every musician learns to play.

The instrument that leads the ensemble is a kind of xylophone called *Ranad Ek*. The keyboard is made of slabs of hardwood or bamboo graduated in length and strung on a cord. The keyboard, in turn, is attached to a boat-shaped frame by hanging the cord on hooks on the end-pieces, somewhat like a hammock. The frame is often carved and highly decorated. The player uses two mallets which are long, thin sticks of bamboo with padded ends. In ensembles the instrument plays a variation of melodies. When it is used as a solo instrument, the music is often more melodic and complicated. Often the hands of skillful players move so quickly that one cannot see them clearly.

Another type of xylophone, called *Ranad Thong Thume*,

*A traditional Thai musical ensemble is made up of
players on percussion, string, and wind instruments.*

lower in pitch, has the same kind of keyboard. Its case is a
long box instead of the curved boat-shaped stand. Some
xylophones — the ones used only in large ensembles —
have metal keys that rest on top of the case instead of
hanging from a cord.

The rhythm instruments are of two kinds — drums and
cymbals. Some drums are only used in the large ensembles.
These drums are barrel-shaped, about two-and-one-half
feet high, and are called *Klong Thad*. They are struck with
large, heavy bamboo sticks in a steady syncopated pattern.
The sound is similar to the Western kettledrum.

The most important drum is a smaller, barrel-shaped
drum called the *Tapone* which rests on a wooden stand.
It is considered the "spiritual" leader of the group. A good

player can produce as many as eleven sounds on it, playing on both heads with both his hands. When it is played with many complex patterns it gives variety to the rhythmic structure of the ensemble. It also helps keep all of the players together since there is no conductor.

In informal playing the composition of the playing group changes. Instead of the drum mentioned, a pair of long, narrow drums may be used instead. Each of these narrow drums is played by one man who holds a drum on his lap. The two drums are played by hand in complex, interlocking patterns. As the style is informal, the two drummers often carry on a contest, each trying to outdo the other in creating complicated rhythms, each trying to confuse the other, causing him to make a mistake. This is great fun, and the players often call out to one another.

The most important cymbals are paired; made of heavy metal, they are connected by a cord fastened into the top of each. They are called *Charb*. The cymbals are played by one person, in one of three main patterns — one pattern is slow or long-spaced, another twice as fast, and the third twice as fast as the second. The sweet, chiming sounds of these cymbals occur at regular intervals. Practically all traditional music, both instrumental and vocal, uses one or more of these cymbal patterns as its basic rhythmic design. All Thai music is of a two-beat structure.

Among the wind instruments are bamboo flutes and three instruments made of hardwood. These latter are played with a double reed. They sound something like an oboe. One Thai "oboe" has a conical shape; similar instruments may be found all over Asia. In Thailand it is used to accompany Thai boxing and old-style hand-to-hand combat exhibitions. The harsh, strident tone is a suitable background for these rough sports.

Two of the stringed instruments, similar to ones found in China, have two strings between which the bow is fastened so that it cannot be removed. These instruments have unfretted round necks. The sound box of one, made from a section of a large bamboo, is open at one end and is covered at the other with skin, on which rests a bridge that supports the strings. The other instrument is much the same, except that the body is made of half a coconut shell.

There is also a large, three-stringed zither about a yard long, with a narrow boxlike body and an oblong head which in the old days was carved like a crocodile. The instrument is still called a "crocodile" by the Thai. It rests on the floor and the strings are plucked by the player. It was once very popular with court ladies, who played it as a solo instrument, their arms moving gracefully.

The tuning of Thai instruments is different from that of the West. The space of the octave is divided into seven equal parts. Most Thai tunes are based on five tones, the other two decorate the melody. One instrument plays the main melody, other instruments play variations; complicated rhythms weave these strands together. The different sounds of the instruments also add variety, some giving a plaintive undertone even to lively tunes. A Thai listens to one of the lines of variation which flows against the main melody for a while, then turns his attention to another.

There is no written system of notation for Thai music; it has always been learned by ear. Tunes were passed down from one generation to another and carried around the country by musicians who often knew hundreds of tunes by heart. When a boy wished to become a musician, he went to a teacher and stayed for years, learning all the pieces that his teacher knew. In this way, traditional music has come down through the centuries.

In traditional music, singing is never accompanied by the instruments; sections of singing alternate with sections of instrumental music. As the language is tonal, the notes of the melody of the singing part must match the tonal movement of the words. Between the words, meaningless syllables are often sung to which any melody can be used, giving variety to the songs. The style of Thai singing is considered by some Westerners as nasal, but this style is admired by the Thai and much time is spent in learning it.

In country districts, Thai music is still an important part of daily life. Here the folk music is simpler than the high art music of the city. Folk music and songs are usually shorter and faster than classical music. There are songs that tell of the exploits of heroes. There are ballads and love songs, and duets in which a girl and a boy sing alternate couplets. There are lullabies, boat songs, and songs that accompany work. And today, young people in both the city and villages are often heard singing movie songs or those from popular Western recordings.

The instruments used by countrypeople are simpler than those used in classical music. In the villages, music is always an inseparable part of ceremonies and functions.

The most popular folk instrument of northern Thailand looks like a set of large Panpipes and sounds like a mouth organ. Small metal reeds are placed inside thin tubes of bamboo which are attached to a mouthpiece. Each tube has a small hole through which the air can escape. When the hole is closed by a finger tip, the reed makes a sound. The instrument is made in many sizes, some as large as seven feet. They are all made by hand, as are all instruments in Thailand, and the tuning varies from one instrument to another. They are used to accompany songs and dances or for solos. People often play one of the smaller pipes as they go to work along mountain trails. It helps a man to forget the heavy burdens he carries on his back, and heartens him if he thinks of dangers that might befall. Echoing thinly across the valleys, in a sad, minor key, the music sounds as though it were played by a mountain spirit.

Large conch shells are blown like trumpets at ceremonies of Brahman origin, as they were, and still are, blown in India. The shell belongs to a rare species which opens to the right instead of to the left as the common variety does. They were once much in demand and very costly, eagerly sought by divers in the seas north of Ceylon. The conch shells were often decorated with designs in gold and jewels. Before the change in government there were many colorful ceremonies in which conch shells were blown. These ceremonies are rarely seen today.

It is a good thing that an effort is being made to keep the old music alive. It would be a great loss if it should disappear entirely from the life of the country.

13

The Show Goes On

"To make a good show conceal the end of the thread."

The Thai love a show of any kind. Movies are very popular all over Thailand and are shown regularly in every big town. In the dry season, traveling tent moving-picture shows go to the small villages where the roads are solid enough for the trucks. During the rainy season they cannot use the side roads which are rivers of mud.

Brightly dressed and smiling, the Thai crowd into the show: men, women, chattering children; and babies slung on their mothers' hips. They bring refreshments with them — fruit, sticky sweetmeats, or dried melon seeds. Hawkers shoulder their way through the aisles while the show is on, selling bottles of gaily-colored pop. The audience munches and sips its way through the performance.

The earliest form of theatrical show given in Thailand, mentioned in texts written in 1458, was called *nang*. The name means "leather" and comes from the large, cutout figures of leather that were used in the show. The shadows of the figures fall on a white cloth screen which is lighted from behind. (The Thai call the movies nang, too, for the movies are shadows which move across a screen.)

In early days, the light was furnished by a fire or pitch torches, but later an acetylene lantern was used, and sometimes today the light is electricity. The long, high screen is made of thin, white cloth doubled at the ends in order to hide the entrances and exits of the figures.

The leather used in the true nang is heavy and stiff. The figures are mounted on two long bamboo sticks fastened near each side. The figures are in one piece and not jointed. They are five feet tall and may be several feet wide. The shapes are elaborately cut in the leather with a knife, and perforations in the design allow the light to shine through parts of the shadow. The characters are surrounded by decorative designs or conventional foliage and flowers all attached together as in a stencil.

Sometimes the performance is put on before dark. Then the nang is held in front of the screen. The figures for these are painted in beautiful colors and fine detail. Many of the old ones are so handsome, they are kept in the Art Museum in Bangkok.

During the performance a man moves the nang about, holding the ends of the sticks on which they are mounted. He raises the figures high above his head. At night, the nang are held close to the screen so that the shadows will be distinct. The man wears a jacket and a fancy panung draped about his legs and held with a sash. On his head is a small turban. As he moves the nang to and fro, the man poses with his arms and legs in time to the music in a stylized imitation of the character shown. At the same time, a story from Thai literature is recited. The man jumps about drolly when showing monkeys, moves gracefully for the feminine figures, and takes strong, manly poses for the heroes or combatants.

A performance needs many figures. They are kept piled in sets in back of the screen, arranged in order so that they will be at hand for the action of the story. An army or pro-

cession may cross the screen, carried by many manipulators. When the manipulators reach the end of the screen, they pass in back of the light to return again.

If disease visited a village, the nang players used to be called in to help exorcise the troublesome spirits. The chief part in the play would be that of an especially evil spirit. It was expected that the demons causing the sickness would be curious and would come to see the show. Then, recognizing a master more powerful than themselves, they would slink away, dispirited.

These superstitions have vanished today. Nang plays, once so prevalent that they were carried all over the country by strolling companies, are only occasionally given at fairs or in the courtyard of a wat.

It is thought that the nang performers, with their stylized posturing, developed into the classical dance-drama. Performed by living actors, the dance-drama is still played in the style of former centuries. The costumes are very similar to the ceremonial garb once worn by Thai royalty; stage gods and kings wear the same high, peaked crowns, and magnificent garments embroidered with gold. Imitation jewels and bits of brilliant mirror twinkle on the players' bright costumes of cloth woven with gold thread and brilliant colors. The players' arms glitter with many bracelets and, as they glide back and forth, their anklets clink together.

Many of the plays are taken from the *Ramakien*. These stories relate the adventures of Prince Rama. His father wished him to be heir to the throne, but the beautiful second queen persuaded the king to grant her a boon. She then told him that she wished Rama to be exiled and her own son made heir in his place. The king had to keep his promise, so Rama left the kingdom and went to live in the forest. He was accompanied by his faithful wife, Sita.

There were many evil beings in the forest and the brave Rama fought and conquered them. Their ruler, the demon king Ravana, swore revenge. He sent a demon down in the form of a deer to entice Rama into the depths of the forest on a hunt. While Rama was away, Ravana carried off Sita to his kingdom. When Rama returned and could not find his wife, he wandered about the forest seeking her. He met an eagle who had been wounded by Ravana and the eagle told him what had happened.

Rama waged war against Ravana, and was joined by the monkey people, under their leader, Hanuman. After countless events, Rama rescued Sita and was restored to his throne.

The story is so long and so embellished only a small part of it can be acted at one time.

Male dancers in khon enact a duel between a demon (right) and Hanuman, the king of the monkeys (left).

A performance must not end with a tragedy. If the hero is wounded or worsted in a fight, the story must continue until all is right again.

Stage heroes and gods once wore crowned masks that covered the entire head. Now they wear only the crown. Each distinctive type of crown represents a different character. The demons and monkeys still wear masks. There are hundreds of styles of masks, differing in design and color for leaders, the rank and file of armies, and various characters. The monkey king has a white face and his mask has a domed crown. The mask of the demon king has a green face. He was said to have ten faces, so the mask has three diminishing heads, one above the other, and the middle head has four faces.

The types of faces of the monkeys and demons differ, too. A monkey's mouth may be open or closed. Some demons have a snarling mouth, some "clamp their teeth" inside an angry, turned-down mouth. Some have terrible tusks. Their eyes may bulge or resemble those of a crocodile. Characters are also told apart by the weapons that they carry: tridents, daggers, lances, bows, or clubs.

The female characters, princesses, and celestial beings, used to have their faces covered with thick, white paint made of chalk. Red lips and black eyebrows were painted on. They showed no expression, for the paint might crack if they moved their features. Today their make-up is more natural, and they can smile and show some expression. Such strong contrast is not needed now that theatrical lighting is so much brighter.

The dressing of a dancer used to be a long, tiring affair. The garments had to be sewed onto the performer so they would not slip during the strenuous action of the dance. It might be nearly two hours before a dancer was ready. Now the costumes are arranged to go on more easily; it does not take half the time to dress, and often the performers help one another. The folds of the garments are sewed together before they are put on, and they have tapes to tie them in place. Zippers are used wherever possible. The lower garment is held in place by a band of cotton tied tightly around the hips, then covered with a sash or belt. The costumes are laid out behind the scenes, ready for the dancers. Wooden stands hold the heavy metal crowns and painted masks.

Figurines dressed like dancers and models of masks, both miniature and life size, are sold in shops. They are intended for decorations. Among the children's toys are crude papier-mâché masks which the children wear when they play at acting.

Masks and thick make-up prevent the actors from speaking their parts. A chorus recites the story and speaks dialogue for the actors; they sing at the more emotional moments of the story.

The music helps to carry the story. There are walking, marching, or fighting tunes, some for sorrow, love, or anger. The audience knows what each tune means and is ready with the right emotion when an action starts.

There are also traditional gestures, each with a distinctive meaning. Actors representing men or women use different sets of gestures to indicate the same emotions. For instance, a girl shows displeasure by touching her chin with the palm of her turned-back hand; an angry man points his finger and stamps a foot. When he is ambitious he stiffens his body. When he makes love to a girl, he touches her cheek gently with his fingers, while she sways toward him, her hand with outspread fingers against her body, the other arm curved away from him in feigned reluctance. An actor can show the wind swaying the tops of the trees with his hands; or a graceful pose while looking upward shows that the moon is there. A god with four arms is indicated by one actor posing behind another, their arms gesturing together. There is endless variety.

There are two forms of drama, *khon* and *lakhon*. Khon is the older form and only men act in it, for it is very strenuous. There is much vigorous fighting and clashing of weapons. Acrobatic actors, representing monkeys, somer-

sault back and forth across each other in perfect timing.
A fighter may pose on one leg, standing on the bent knee
of an opponent, showing him to be the victor. The actors
make huge leaps from imaginary cliffs.

Lakhon is more gentle and graceful than khon, and is
acted only by women. The muscular postures of khon are
replaced by gliding, swaying, dancing motions. The sinu-
ous arms of the actresses move back and forth bonelessly.
The backs of their hands bend outward towards the wrists

A love scene in lakhon is played by female dancers
who take the roles of both the "hero" and "heroine".

in a curve. The costumes are much the same in both forms of the drama, but masks are not worn for lakhon.

Many of the stories for lakhon come from Thai folklore, and some stories have been written especially for it. There are few modern plays, however, for it is hard to adapt them to the formal gestures. As with our opera, mostly the old ones are performed.

Lakhon was once acted only in the king's palace. As each performer came into the king's presence, she bowed low to the floor before him, then rose to take part in the show. As the performers were all female, the court ladies could be present to watch. The women's quarters in the palace were called the "inside," and so lakhon came to be known as the "drama of the inside."

King Rama III (1824-1851) considered the dance too frivolous and would not have it performed in the palace. Princes and nobles dared to have lakhon given at their palaces and took over the troupes of dancers who had been under the patronage of the king. Shows were often given out of doors or in courtyards. Guests were invited to watch and the public could see it from a respectful distance. There was no scenery.

Often today there is no scenery on stage. There are only a few props. A long, low bench may represent a throne. A bed may be a boat or the back of an elephant, or it might represent a cloud for the gods. Sometimes a screen is put up to indicate a room, or a few plants in pots can represent a forest. Sometimes a real, carved chariot is drawn onto the stage, or figures sit beneath a royal canopy or pavilion.

Performances of khon and lakhon are sponsored by the Department of Fine Arts, and on special occasions scenery and elaborate props are used. When Hanuman the monkey king wishes to save Rama's army, he swallows them. They march into the gaping mouth of a huge, artificial head. Fire is represented by red-silk flames, fluttering in the breeze of an offstage electric fan. A magician calls forth lovely maidens from a huge cauldron set on skulls. Formerly all these actions would have been told by gestures, recitations, and music.

Many Thai prefer a loud and noisy form of comedy called *likay*. In these comedies, the actors sing and speak their own parts in an individual style to please themselves. The audience laughs loudly at the rough humor of the clowns, and shouts its approval of topical jokes, which are often spontaneous.

When the play is over at midnight, the people stream out into the quiet street, still laughing and talking about the show. They tug along sleepy children and carry baskets that had contained food. The lights go out in the hall, leaving it silent until morning when cleaners sweep up the litter of paper and fruit skins.

The Department of Fine Arts runs an academy where courses in dancing and dramatics are given. It takes ten years to become a finished performer. Girls and boys start to learn when they are eight years old and their bodies are highly flexible.

Children are selected to be trained for only one type of part. The girls learn to be heroes and heroines, and the boys learn to be monkeys, demons, and other strenuous roles. The classes are taught separately in a large, cool room which has many windows opening on a garden. The floor is polished and there is a small stage at one end.

The preliminary students are barefooted during the classes and wear red panungs and white blouses or shirts. When the girls enter the room, the "heroes" go to one side and the "heroines" to the other. Sometimes they sit on the floor while they practice arm and torso exercises, learning rhythm and flexibility. They chant the time in unison. A former dancer is the teacher for each group. The teachers watch carefully, correcting the movements of the children.

The girls stand to combine arm gestures with leg movements, learning dancing and walking steps. Those of the male characters are different from those of the female characters. The heroines must be more graceful.

The parts taught the boys are far more strenuous than those of the girls. The "demons" are set apart from the "monkeys." Some of the preliminary training is the same

Older students are taught singly or in small groups. A few may be chosen for the classical theater in Bangkok.

for each group. Some exercises teach rhythm and flexibility, others strengthen bodies and legs for the acrobatic motions. Male teachers clack bamboo sticks together to keep the time, or to tap a boy to correct the position of an arm or leg. The boys pose on one leg with the other in the air, then move along the floor on the one standing leg. They stamp their feet rhythmically, jarring the room. They tramp along with small steps, knees bent, toes turned out, feet slapping the floor vigorously. A boy must learn to spread his legs out to each side, parallel to his body. He stands against the wall while a teacher sits on the floor in front of him. The teacher stretches out his legs and pushes with his feet against the boy's knees, flattening the student's legs against the wall.

A "monkey's" training is even more rigorous. He must learn to leap about, walk on his hands, turn somersaults. He puts the palms of his hands and the soles of his feet on the floor at the same time — either face or back upwards. Then he flips over into a standing position.

The children practice for three hours a day. After the lessons are over, they scamper out for lunch. Between dancing lessons they are taught the usual school curriculum.

The older students are taught singly or in small groups. A few musicians, seated on the stage, keep time for them. They are taught sets of dance gestures and movements that are fitted together for a performance.

Many of the graduates will teach dancing in small cities and towns of Thailand. They may give performances in these places on special occasions. A few will be accepted for the classical theater in Bangkok. In this way, the old arts are able to flourish and are kept fresh and alive.

14

The Thai Enjoy Themselves

"A blanket keeps away the cold wind, and a happy heart drives out sadness."

The pleasure-loving Thai do not need a movie or a theatrical show, much as they enjoy them. They make their own fun if there is no organized pleasure. Almost anything can be *sanuck*, the Thai word for a cheerful good time. They relieve arduous work by laughing and joking together, so it becomes sanuck, too.

The friendly Thai enjoy being in the company of others. It is impossible to imagine a Thai playing solitaire. They are always ready for a party and enjoy games, either as a player or cheering onlooker. Loud music adds to the fun, and it may be furnished by a phonograph, radio, a band, or someone who plays and sings to a stringed instrument.

There are many religious holidays with traditional forms of entertainment as well as religious rites. These are still kept up, although the meanings of some of the ceremonies may be lost.

Thailand now uses the Western calendar. According to the old reckoning, New Year starts in April at the time of the full moon and lasts for three days. Everything must be clean for the New Year: clothes are washed, houses scrubbed, and all trash cleared away and burned.

The abbot of the temple takes a ceremonial bath and monks sprinkle water on the image of Buddha. Libations of water are poured on the ground. Not only is the water a symbol of purification, but it also encourages plenty of rain for the crops in the coming year. There is a service at the temple. The monks chant a blessing: "May no danger from the real or unreal come to men, to four-footed or two-footed creatures, and may rain fall plentifully over the land." The congregation, carrying bowls of water, walks behind the row of monks, sprinkling them with the water.

The younger people of the village visit the older ones, pour a little scented water into the outspread hands of those to whom they wish to show respect, and receive a blessing in return.

Then the fun begins. Young people and children throng the village streets, each with a container of water. Laughing and joking, they toss it on anyone they meet in a friendly contest. Each tries to be the first to douse the other. Soon everyone is soaking wet, and the rainy season will be a good one.

During this festival, called *Songkran*, there are songs, games, dancing, and music. No one does any unnecessary work.

In the autumn, at the end of the rainy season, the work of planting the rice is over, and the crop is not ready for the harvest. The Thai have time to enjoy the Festival of Lights, called *Loi Kratong*. The village is decorated with streamers, palm fronds, lights, gay paper lanterns, and candles.

After services at the temple, as the big, yellow full moon climbs above the trees into the darkening sky, the people gather on the banks of the rivers and canals. They bring kratong boats with them. These are made of inch-thick slices cut from the stalk of a banana tree. Strips of the leaf are folded about the rim in various shapes to resemble boats or lotus flowers. Some may be hand-carved boats with animal figureheads, others look like airplanes. Often children bring toy boats, bought at the markets. Each kratong contains an offering of a stick of incense, a candle, flowers, and a small coin. The candles and incense are lighted, then the kratong are carefully set adrift in the water, with a prayer that last year's sins may be carried away with them.

The ceremony is older than Buddhism, and was probably started to placate the water spirit and to ask pardon for polluting the water. Some people still think that this ceremony will insure against death by drowning. Others recall the legend of the Nagas, the huge serpents that leap about in a lake in the mythical land of the gods, spouting water which brings the rain. The king of the Nagas asked Buddha to leave his footprint in a river so that it might be there as a memorial after the Master had attained nirvana. The kratong are set afloat to atone for possibly passing over these prints in boats.

The kratong drift on the water, like hundreds of floating stars. They silently sail over the reflections of the real stars. The ripples bob the boats along, while their owners watch, hoping the tiny boats will not capsize. The further they float safely, the more auspicious it is. The children, who have been preparing their boats for days, look forward to sending them on the journey to the larger rivers. They feel a little wistful as the kratong drift out of sight, but soon there will be fireworks.

Traveling about the country is a great pleasure for young and old. Going on pilgrimages to famous temples is an act of merit, and as much a picnic as a religious duty. Often these excursions are made at the same time that holiday fairs are held at the temple, mixing the religious observances and secular fun. The pilgrimage might be to Phrabat, where there is a footprint of Buddha in the rock, or to Phra Pathom, where there is a Phra Chedi — a spire 375 feet high, which stands on the oldest religious site in Thailand, nearly a thousand years old. It may be to any temple that contains a relic of Buddha, or an especially revered figure of him.

The fairs last three days and raise funds to keep the temples in repair. Outside the walls that surround the temple, shows are held: nang, Thai dancers, or Chinese theater which goes on indefinitely and monotonously to squeaking stringed instruments and banging gongs in a high booth. There may be a small, rickety-looking Ferris wheel spinning slowly on bamboo struts. The tootle of a snake charmer's horn attracts an ever-widening circle of fascinated observers. When the performer, with a torpid

snake draped about his neck, thinks there are enough people and a good collection of coins, he starts the show, using
the snakes he keeps in a basket.

In the country districts there are displays of agricultural

products and local handicrafts, with prizes for the best. Temporary booths, both outside and inside the temple grounds, are erected under matting or cloth awnings and are decorated with strips of red cloth. Over the passageways between them are strips of cloth to provide shelter from the sun. The cloth is tied by ropes to the wat buildings and to the colored spires of Phra Chedis that rise above the tawdry booths.

Bands play and radios screech from the booths to call attention to the goods displayed. There is something to suit every taste — silk scarfs, sandals, and clothing hang from curved strips of bamboo; plastic combs, inexpensive jewelry and beads, and bottles of strong scent are temptingly shown. Tinware and dishes are sold. So are baskets, some made of openwork plastic, distressingly bright in color. Children look longingly at toys: bright woven paper fish or birds attached to the end of a flexible rattan strip to keep them bobbing, papier-mâché dolls, imitations of theater masks to fit over the head, animals painted in impossible colors, plastic models of autos, and tin mechanical toys. Masses of balloons sway in the air above the children's heads. Even those children with no money to spend can stand around and stare happily.

Boys gather around a shooting gallery, waving guns wildly while they await their turn. Then they lean so far across the counter that they nearly push the target with the gun muzzles as they compete for flimsy prizes. They play Ping-pong. On a wooden floor inside a tent, they scurry about on velocipedes, colliding with each other.

A little girl does none of these things, but wanders about gazing, with a baby on her hip. Both are eating. She may have bought sweets from a peddler who carries a pole topped with a mass of straw, into which the candies are stuck at the ends of sticks, or maybe a round of sugar cane which was pinned to a length of bamboo.

A Chinese vendor is surrounded by children. His portable wooden stand holds a dripping cake of ice. For a small coin, he scrapes a mushy bit into a small folded banana-leaf and adds a dash of sweet sirup of some violent color. The children lap it up.

Everywhere there is a smell of food — spicy, greasy, fishy — from booths or portable kitchens; these kitchens joggle from both ends of a pole which rests on the peddler's shoulder as he follows the crowd to the most popular events. The peddler may squat near a gambling game. The odds are strongly against the players. The prizes are cheap trash, or a few cents worth of coins. A cloth spread on the counter is divided into squares. Each contains the picture of an animal. Each better tosses a coin onto his favorite. When the banker thinks he has as many dupes as possible, he spins a hand on an upright disk with the same animals depicted around its outer edge. The hand clacks around a few times, then stops. Those who bet on the winning animal press forward, pleased to have won any sort of prize.

In the next booth, thin cords are passed through a hollow length of bamboo. Some are attached to prizes. A man pays his money, then selects a string to pull. The chances are that it comes free with nothing attached — certainly not any of the finer objects displayed. Dart games, hoopla, and bingo also provide ways to lose some money.

All day long streams of people go in and out of the temple. They pass by women squatting by baskets, selling tuberoses or lotus, candles, incense, and thin, inch-square sheets of gold leaf. These are offerings for the Buddha. Old nuns dressed in white robes sit half-asleep on the steps of the building. They are in charge of large wax candles, the sides of which bristle with coins, a contribution from the devout.

Inside, away from the clang of gongs and the blare of music, it is dusky and peaceful, with only the droning voices of monks chanting scriptures. After a reverent obeisance, a worshiper leaves his offering and slips out again from the incense-smelling stillness into the din, heat, and glare of the fair.

The festivities keep on late into the night. The booths are transformed by twinkling lights into pools of magic. Cornices and the tops of spires catch the light and seem to float on the shadows, gleaming against the black sky. After a burst of fireworks streaks colored stars across the heavens, the crowd drifts homewards, carrying purchases and prizes, with worn-out children tagging along. The music and noise are finished.

Competitive games take place on many national holidays and religious festivals during the year. Among the patriotic holidays is Constitution Day, the date when the first Thai constitution was signed and the country changed from an absolute monarchy. The king's birthday is celebrated; and a day is dedicated to King Chulalongkorn, Thailand's best-beloved monarch. On Chakri Day, the kings of the present dynasty are honored.

Many Western sports have been introduced. Competitions take place in the National Stadium, and games are played on school grounds — foot races, javelin throwing, tennis, basketball played out of doors, and soccer — are all very popular Thai sports. Soccer appeals naturally to the Thai for it has some of the features of a national game called *takraw*, which is played informally or as a contest throughout the country, the year around.

Several players knock a hollow wicker ball, slightly larger than a baseball, back and forth between them, without touching it with the hands. The players leap and twist about, dexterously keeping the ball flying from one to another, striking it with the head, shoulders, elbows, or bare feet. Any part of the body may be used except the hands.

In March, when the wind piles masses of clouds high into the sky, forerunners of the rainy season, kiteflying competitions begin. Kiteflying is not only an amusement but a competitive sport, often between kiteflying experts. An umpire watches the flight carefully and renders decisions on fine points of the contest. He also limits the number of kites that can compete at any one time.

Two types of kites are used in the contest: a big *chula*, the male, and a much smaller *pakpao*, the female. They

are both made of tough paper stretched on bamboo frames. The chula is about seven feet high, somewhat star-shaped, with five points. It has a series of hooks high on its cord that are used in attack to catch the cord or the tail of the pakpao. It tugs so strongly that it takes a team of several men to handle it in flight. The pakpao is in the form of a rhomboid, with a tail made of starched cotton cloth. The object of the contest is for one kite to obstruct or entangle the other, causing it to lose its balance and plunge down to earth. Although the chula is much heavier, the pakpao is more maneuverable; even so, it gains twice as many points as the chula does if it wins in the fight. National contests are held in Bangkok on the large open space in front of the white wall that encloses the royal palace and temples.

On buses, autos, bicycles, or on foot, the crowd gathers, and scatters across the field. They cheer their favorites, and often bet on the outcome of the fights as they watch the kites twisting and darting overhead. They burst into whoops of glee or outrage when a kite drops. All day long the contests go on. Peddlers of food and sweet drinks do a thriving business. Finally, the evening sky turns orange and pink behind the gilded spires and glowing roofs of the palace. The setting sun stains the palace with even more incandescent color than its daytime splendor.

It has all been very sanuck indeed.

15

Weaving

"When buying fabric, examine the material from which it is made."

Old Thai legends tell of princesses sitting at their looms weaving fine silk fabrics as Penelope did while she waited for the return of Ulysses in the old Greek tale.

Weaving of silk and cotton were home industries. Nearly every farmer's wife had a loom. When her work in the fields was finished for the year, after the harvest of the rice crop, the farmer's wife made cloth, mostly of cotton. She sold what was not needed for the family's garments. Much home weaving is still done in Thailand.

A loom is kept in the shaded place beneath the house, where the breeze blows coolly, rattling the fronds of the nearby palms. The mother or grandmother sits working at the loom while a daughter sits on the ground, spinning thread on a homemade wooden wheel worked by hand. She feeds in the cotton which she takes from a basket beside her. The younger children have rolled the fluffy cotton between their hands into twelve-inch lengths.

Chickens peck about at crumbs which fell through the cracks in the floor above with the morning's sweeping. The pig dozes in a shallow hollow he has made in the ground, dusty and comfortable. Babies crawl about. If one stumbles and cries, there is time to stop work and comfort him, or to push a little cold rice or banana into his mouth. It is all easy and friendly. Working hours in a factory would not please the average Thai, but some girls do work in factories in Bangkok today. Thai in the towns and cities prefer cotton cloth that has been woven and printed in factories. They say that home-woven cotton is coarse and of uneven quality.

The cloth intended for *pasins*, the folded skirts, is woven in plaids or stripes, with a plain border that forms the end of the garment. Some cloth is printed with large floral or small, allover designs. There were once distinctive designs traditional to each part of the country, which were changed to some extent by the worker to suit her own taste. These patterns were carved in relief on wide hardwood boards, and different dyes were applied to the various parts of the design. The board was the size of the piece of material, and did the whole job at one printing. Vegetable dyes made from flowers, berries, barks, and grasses were used.

Yellow dye comes from the wood of a tree cut in chips and boiled. This is now used to dye monks' robes. The yellow varies through all the colors of a marigold, from orange-brown to golden yellow. Blue comes from the indigo plant; this is mixed with yellow to make green. Sticlac, which furnishes many different reds, is a waxy incrustation formed by insects that suck the sap of trees; when the wax is removed, a sediment remains which is the dye. When sticlac dye is fresh, the color obtained is brick-red. The color varies with the age of the sticlac — scarlet, pink, and crimson. The dye is violet when the sticlac is a year old.

A fine black dye is obtained from a berry. It is fast and rich, but cannot be exported, as it can only be used when freshly gathered. China sends woven cloth to Thailand to be dyed black and returned. In front of dark sheds where the vats of dye steam are bamboo racks, thirty feet high. Men in black shorts, hands and arms weirdly stained, hang the wide banners of gloomy cloth. It seems as though they are preparing for some giant's funeral.

Chemical dyes are mostly used today. There would not be enough vegetable dyes for large quantities of material, and most of the vegetable dyes are not fast in color. The chemical dyes are more accurate, and it is easier to keep the colors uniform when mixed in large amounts for the silk which is exported from Thailand.

A great deal of silk was once woven, when the upper-class men as well as women wore garments of silk. The nobles wore heavy silk panungs, made of a length of material draped between the legs. The material was woven with intricate patterns of gold thread. The nobles wore a thin silk tunic embroidered with gold and with jeweled buttons. The women wore a pasin or a panung, with a scarf draped about the shoulders.

With the influence of Western dress the silk industry declined, but today it is again flourishing. This is chiefly due to the efforts of Jim Thompson who was an American army officer in World War II. After the war, he came to Bangkok to live. He saw some lengths of Thai silk in a small shop. It was so beautiful and so fine in quality that it made him think that silk weaving could be a profitable industry.

He searched through the countryside for weavers, encouraged them to work in their homes, financed them, and supervised their work. He soon had a big business under way. Others came into the field, and today woven silk is one of Thailand's biggest exports and has brought prosperity to its workers. There are agencies for the silk in twenty-six different countries.

The Government, in turn, has encouraged the cultivation of silkworms and has started sericulture stations to give silkworm eggs and mulberry slips to the people.

The eggs are laid by small, yellow moths, and hatch into tiny larvae. The larvae must feed on mulberry leaves constantly. The farmer and his family are kept busy supplying them both day and night. After weeks of endless crunching, the worms have tripled in size, and they stop eating. They begin to move about restlessly. They are then placed in a large, flat wicker basket which contains a spiral of rattan. The worms form cocoons in the grooves. The silk as it comes from the mouths of the worms is a sticky fluid which becomes thready filaments when it reaches the air. Before the moth can escape from the cocoon and injure the filaments, the cocoons are placed in hot water in a large pot. In minutes, the gummy substance that covers the cocoons partly dissolves and the ends float free in the water. The worker stirs the water gently with a small wooden paddle, and the ends of the filaments stick to this. Several strands are loosened from the paddle and passed through a small reel which hangs over the pot. The gumminess causes the filaments to stick together and to form a raw silk thread. It takes nearly three thousand cocoons to make one pound of silk.

Most of the raw silk is sent to Bangkok. In the outskirts there is a small village of silkworkers. It seems another world, away from the brisk, noisy city. Life goes on at a much slower pace in the small houses of gray, weathered wood and palm thatch, which stretch along the banks of a canal. On the water front boards make a pathway from house to house, crossing landings where each family's sampan is moored. Runways of boards lead along narrow alleys between the houses, above water when the tide is high and on mud when the tide is out. Eaves almost touch and sunlight flickers down through the leaves of trees and palms, lighting up hanging pots of bright orchids, or turning a bunch of silk skeins to fire as they glow with crimson, scarlet, orange, and gold. Runaway bits of gay silk fluff stick to the rough edges of the boards.

The clickety-clack of looms comes from the houses or from the platforms beneath them. People work on the wood runways and on covered platforms as they degum raw silk or dye it. They can look up from their work to watch the busy life on the canal. Boats pass, carrying merchandise to sell — anything from clay jars to alarm clocks or fruit: yellow bananas, orange pineapples, and small, ripe oranges of a deep green color. Vegetable women cry their wares: eggplants, pearly onions, dark red chilies, and cool green Chinese cabbage. All these hues seem to have spilled into the water from the gaily colored skeins of dyed silk hanging on bamboo racks in front of the houses.

The raw silk is harsh with gum and golden in color. It must be soaked in hot water and soda to remove the gum that permeates it, then rinsed in fresh water. Trails of wet, yellow gum stain the board platforms and form runnels in the mud and ditches. The silk is now a creamy white. After drying, it is spun into even skeins on wooden reels, turned by hand by a woman who sits on the floor. The reels are homemade, and vary somewhat in design.

When reeled, the skeins are ready for the dyers. First they are weighed and tied in bundles, as the amount of dye used is regulated by the weight of the silk so that the final color will be uniform. Chemical dyes are used, mixed

*A worker winds silk thread in a small village. When
reeled, the skeins are ready for the next step — dyeing.*

to reproduce many of the old natural-dye colors. A book of
sample tufts of colored silk is kept by the head worker,
each with the correct formula for the dye to be used.

The dyers' garments are dappled with as many colors as
a modernistic painting. They heat the dye mixture in a
kerosene can over a small clay stove. (These large, useful
cans, with the top removed, serve as buckets all over
Thailand.) The coils of silk hang from strips of bamboo,
bent to the shape of a horseshoe. When the silk has become the color desired, it is washed in the canal to remove
the excess color. The washerwoman squats on the wooden
steps leading down from the landing.

The silk is then hung on racks to dry, some with the
colors of a sunset — fiery reds, pinks, orange, or violet —

some with soft, muted colors. As in the sunset, the brightest colors never seem to clash.

Sometimes the threads of the warp are tied tightly together in a pattern of knots before it is dyed. The part that is tied does not take the color, and shows up as a design when the silk is woven.

Next the thread is reeled on bobbins for the weavers, one thread or more twisted together according to the weight of silk desired. It should be soft and thin for dress goods and scarves, heavier for drapery material, or sturdy for upholstery fabrics. The bobbins are placed in baskets or on racks, ready for the weavers.

The loom consists of a horizontal frame supported by uprights. It is worked by foot treadles that alternately raise and separate a series of the threads of the warp so the bobbins can pass through. A girl sits on a low seat slung from the loom, reaching across it and managing all the different bobbins used in the design, pushing the weft firmly into place.

Some households have one or two looms, some a dozen. The girls are paid by the woven yard; so they work as long as they wish, then return to their families.

There are now working drawings for all the intricate patterns that the weaver used to carry in her head. Some silks have stripes, plaids, or repeat designs of conventional forms or flowers; some have bands of varying widths and patterns; and some have crossing threads of different colors, making shot effects.

Often the silk is woven mixed with gold thread. Old gold brocades are very heavy and stiff, but the modern trade wants it supple, so it will fall in graceful folds. After the silk is woven, it is placed on rollers beneath a heavy,

Weaving is a home industry. This weaver sits on a seat slung from her loom which is kept beneath the house.

curved stone. A man holds onto a wooden bar, balancing with a foot on each side of the stone, rocking it back and forth until the material becomes smooth and pliable as it passes across the rollers.

Many stylish Thai ladies wear a different color for each day of the week. Long ago astrologers selected the colors that would be lucky, but now they are only chosen for chic. The order is yellow, pink, green, brown or orange, purple or mauve, and red.

The National Art Museum exhibits clothing of former periods and lengths of cloth with antique designs. Silk or cotton cloth was once, and still is, used for cushion and pad covering, bedding, and mosquito nets as well as for clothing. Curtains were not hung in windows, for they would block the flow of air, though there were some purely decorative hangings of rich materials.

Piles of bright cotton and entrancing silks fill the modern shops on the main streets; or one can seek out a small shop on a narrow lane, its wooden shutters folded back to show the goods in the open interior. The polished floor is a foot or two above street level. Scarves hang on bamboo rods suspended from the ceiling. Many bolts of silk line the walls, filling the small shop with luxury.

At these small shops a tourist can bargain watched by an interested audience in the lane. The price may not be very different in the end from that in the large stores, but it will be part of the fun to remember later on.

16

Kings and Palaces

"Descent determines caste, but demeanor proclaims the man."

During the last hundred years, Bangkok has changed from a medieval town to a large, modern city. Many changes were begun during the reign of King Mongut who came to the throne in 1851 and reigned for seventeen years. He was a progressive monarch, and Thailand under his rule was well on its way to becoming a modern country. He was followed by his son, King Chulalongkorn, who is considered Thailand's greatest ruler. During his reign of forty-one years, King Chulalongkorn furthered the innovations his father had commenced. After him, his sons and grandsons continued the same progressive policies. These kings voluntarily gave up much of their absolute power, and the people had to be educated to accept the changes.

In 1932, during the reign of King Prajadhipok, a group of army officers demanded a parliamentary government and constitution. The populace took no part in these demands but the king had been considering changes in the government for some time, so he was willing to co-operate and signed the new constitution. He said: "My sincere prayer is that the country shall prosper and the people have peace and happiness."

The country became a limited monarchy, and the vote

was granted to everyone — both men and women. A king would still reign, loved and respected, a symbol of the country.

The present king lives in a new palace inside a large park, and his life is very different from that of his predecessors. Former kings of Thailand, when they were absolute monarchs, lived in palace enclosures, which were like fortified towns, within the main city, and massive walls surrounded hundreds of buildings, residences, and temples.

A palace building, erected as a residence for one of the royal princes in 1783, is typical. It has been turned into the National Art Museum and contains the centuries of art. It is built of brick covered with stucco and its walls are two feet thick. There are many rooms covered by tiled Thai roofs similar to those on temple buildings. The whole palace is surrounded by a narrow, colonnaded veranda covered by an extension of the main roof. This furnishes shade to the rooms inside, keeping them cool in the hot weather and warding off driving rain.

There are many windows, without glass, but with wooden shutters painted with figures and designs. These are set in carved frames in deep embrasures. The rooms have high ceilings and they surround courts with formal gardens. Part of the building has an upper story, reached by a double flight of narrow steps. The steps lead to a small landing from which a door opens into the room above.

There was a small chapel in one of the rooms, and another room was a large audience hall which still contains the prince's high throne and other objects used by royalty. The ladies of the prince's court did not live in the palace but in other buildings which are now gone.

The palace enclosure of the kings in Bangkok covers a much larger space, over a square mile in area. Once many thousands of people lived there. The royal palace that stands there today is not an old one. It was built in 1876 for King Chulalongkorn in Italian classic style, but before it was finished, the king decided it should have a Thai roof topped with three spires, so that it would harmonize with the other buildings in the enclosure. Today the old palace and state buildings are used chiefly for functions and ceremonies.

The main wall of the royal enclosure is twelve feet thick; other interior walls divide it into sections. Sentries stand at the huge gate through which elephants once passed. It is called the "Gate of Supreme Victory." One section of the enclosure contains the royal temple, Wat Phra Keo. There are patches of lawn and stone-paved walks lined with tamarind trees, some shaped into cones like those in a child's Noah's ark. In others, the foliage is trimmed into many round balls on twisted branches.

Part of the enclosure once contained all the government ministries, the Court of Justice, barracks of the Royal Guard, an armory, and stables for horses and elephants. The quarters of the royal white elephant were here, too.

Now the work of the government has increased so greatly that the administration buildings and executive offices are outside the palace city. They are on wide avenues and are air-conditioned.

A gate leads through the inner wall to the palace and audience hall, splendidly adorned with rich color and gold. There is a building where the men of the royal household

The palace enclosure of Thai royalty is at Bangkok. The royal temple, Wat Phra Keo, is guarded by a huge demon.

lived, to be at hand to serve the king. There is a theater and the treasury. Each king added to the wealth that was stored away here and seldom seen or admired. It gave a king prestige to own all this splendor of gems, jewelry, crowns, silver, and gold utensils; more things than ever could be used. There were gifts brought by ambassadors from foreign countries and the booty of war. Vassal states sent tribute, including trees made of gold or silver. Some of the trees are seven feet high, with metal-covered trunks set in porcelain stands, and topped by finials. Drooping branches are set in the trunks in nine tiers, about a foot apart. The leaves are serrated and about two inches long. Three-inch flowers are made of two disks, the edges cut into petal shapes, fastened at the center with a domed stud. Other trees are about three feet high and have irregular trunks and branches with smaller leaves and flowers. Some of these gold and silver trees are now in temples as offerings.

Formerly, the king's wish was the final law. No one could touch him. A special dispensation was given to his personal attendants, but they apologized for the liberty with an obeisance. No head could be higher than the king's. Nobles and princes approached him crawling on their knees.

The pride and power of a king were tempered by rules which he was expected to follow — the "Ten Virtues of Monarchs": a king should show charity and give alms, live morally, protect all religions, be honest, be compassionate, have no wrongful ambitions, take no vengeance, be moderate in punishment, love the people like a father, and care for the country's welfare and happiness. It was a truly worthy program when carried out, as much of it often was.

Next to the king's residential quarters, separated by walls, was the women's city, the "inside." At the entrance stood strong, sturdy female guards, carrying arms — the police of the "inside." At night they patrolled the lanes and courts, carrying torches, to insure that all was safe. No man but the king could enter the women's city, except monks who were given permission to enter for religious ceremonies. The monks were escorted by the female guards to the women's temple. Even the king's sons left the inside when they came of age at about nine years old.

The women's city was a maze of courtyards, lanes, and residences for the king's consorts and children and for the princesses and dowager-queens, each with hundreds of ladies in waiting, children's nurses, and slaves. Female administrators, clerks, and treasurers ran the affairs of this city. The noble ladies could not go outside, but sent their maids on errands. They could visit the small shops in the enclosure that sold food, flowers, materials of cotton or silk, toys for the children, candles and offerings for the temple, and many more things.

In the huddled slaves' quarters were women workers, goldsmiths, weavers, gardeners, carpenters, and masons to keep the buildings and furnishings in repair.

The courtyards were charming places and partly made up to the women for their lack of freedom. The yards were paved with marble and shaded by trees. The children watched the goggle-eyed goldfish swim about lazily in pools of water, and the turtles amble. Many flowering plants grew in large porcelain jars. Birds in cages and aviaries attracted the wild birds, and the air was filled with chirping and trilling.

Open salas, beside a tile-lined pool in which the ladies could bathe, gave shelter from the sun. Ornamental bridges joined islands adorned with pagodas and porcelain figures. The ladies sat on carpets, drinking tea and nibbling sweetmeats, as they played games of chance together.

The king's quarters and those of the "inside" were magnificently furnished. Everything the upper classes used was highly ornamented and made to delight the eye. Rugs from Persia and India lay on the floors. Scattered about the floor were flat, padded cushions to sit on, and firmer ones about a foot high, with triangular ends, to lean against. The triangular ones were used on beds also. Beds were made of carved and gilded wood and were fifteen inches high, with wide, flat wooden surfaces attached to the "lion legs" which support so many things in Thailand. These were curved with the claw feet resting on a flattened ball. The bed contained a pad for a mattress and rich coverings. One of the kings had a bed almost like a small house, mounted on the usual bed base, six feet wide and eight feet long. It had a roof supported by carved panels at the corners, decorative brackets and rails at three sides, all carved and adorned with gilt picked out with red.

Tables were benchlike and similar to the flat beds but much smaller. They were low, for the user sat on the floor. Screens, large or small, stood about to give privacy or to keep away drafts in the cool season. Carved frames held panels with designs or figures, either painted in gold and black lacquer, or inlaid with pearl shell. There were some frames folded like Japanese screens and others, like Chinese screens, were mounted between columns which rested on bars with two legs. These screens might be made up of many panels or only one. There were ornamental chests and cabinets to hold clothing or treasures.

The summer palace, near Ayudhya, has been influenced by European architecture but manages to retain a Thai flavor.

One room contained a carved and gilded altar several feet high. It was open on three sides, and before the shelf which held the image of Buddha were a series of smaller shelves to hold offerings.

Attendants wafted long-handled fans to keep the air stirring in the warm season. The spade-shaped surfaces of the fans were embroidered, or made of peacock or some other fine feathers set in a decorative mount. Such fans of dyed chicken or goose feathers may be bought today.

The king gave the ladies generous allowances of money and they dressed in silks and were draped with jewels. Each lady had a low stand with an elaborately framed mirror on it held by brackets. She sat before it to put on her jewelry, to pomade her face, lips, and hair, or to apply perfumes from ceramic jars.

All the ladies were not equally well supplied with money and jewelry for there was a hierarchy of the inside. Royal ladies and consorts especially favored by the king had precedence; the lesser ladies had to bow to the greater.

The king's children by any of the "lady consorts," noble or serving maid, were all recognized by the king as legitimate. The first five kings of the Chakri dynasty had an average of eighty children and forty wives each. It might seem that the country would be full of princes, but the title diminished with each generation until the king's great-great-grandson had no royal title at all. After King Chulalongkorn the kings have been monogamous.

Neither the lady companions nor their children visited the king unless sent for by him. Sometimes the king would give an audience to all the ladies of the palace. They would crouch before him. If any of the young things started to giggle or wriggle about, one of the female guards, whose duty it was to keep order, would reach over and tap her warningly with a rattan.

The women did not speak to the king unless addressed by him. He might ask for news of the inside. Some of the smaller children were present and were allowed a prattling informality. The king, like all the Thai, was fond of children and often petted and fondled them.

Court ladies served meals to the king. One knelt before each large gold or silver tray containing food. One tray was piled with rice; other trays held bowls of soup or curries. There were cakes and sweets protected with wicker domes that were covered with gauzy red silk. One tray was heaped with varieties of fruit, enticingly arranged and ready to eat. The food was so abundant that one person could only have eaten a small part of what was there. When the children were in the presence of the king, they did not eat a meal, but the king might slip them a morsel.

There were twelve kinds of tea, served in as many varieties of teapots: round, squat, many-sided; gold, silver, enameled, or of fine porcelain with gold handles. The teapots were under embroidered silk covers to keep them warm. Some of the tea was scented with flowers, and the strongest was called the "tea of wakefulness."

The king must have needed the tea of wakefulness. His day was a busy one. Descriptions of a monarch's daily life have been left by observers of several reigns. They are all somewhat similar, from the time of King Narai in the seventeenth century until the time of King Mongkut in the nineteenth, when so many traditions were changed.

The king rose early, bathed in water scented with aromatic herbs or crushed flowers, and dressed. Then he gave food personally to the monks who came to the palace on their morning rounds. Next, after a simple breakfast, he went to a service of prayer and meditation in his private chapel. On some days he heard petitions in the outer court presented by his lowlier subjects who could not reach him otherwise. They could come to him to request justice — if they could master a brave-enough spirit. They lay on the ground while a court official presented the plea to the king for his considered opinion. This was a worthy and ancient tradition of the Thai kings from the days of Sukhodaya.

The king held a morning audience for his ministers. Long before the appointed time the nobles arrived. They stood about in the outer court, talking together in muted voices, exchanging rumors, facts, and hopes. Each noble tried to find out the important plans of another and conceal his own — all with great politeness. Before the king was expected, they entered the Great Hall after making a triple obeisance to the door. Dressed in fine silks, they crawled across the floor to a group of red velvet cushions. They took their places before the throne according to rank. When the king was announced by a page carrying the royal insignia — a four-branched candlestick — all became silent and bent their heads to the floor.

The throne was raised on a tapering, tiered pedestal. It had a flat surface, six feet wide, so the king could sit there cross-legged.

During the audience, while he sat on his throne, the king might drink tea or chew betel prepared by a crouching attendant. Another attendant waved a leaf-shaped fan gently, stirring the hot air.

After the audience, the King took his noon meal, then met with the female officials of the inside. After that he relaxed and rested until it was time for another audience with members of the royal family.

Some nights there would be a meeting of the secret council, sometimes lasting throughout the night, where the most important affairs of the kingdom were discussed.

The days and nights were varied according to the wishes of the king, with music by the royal orchestra or performances of the classic drama. The king might go to inspect new buildings under construction in the palace or wats. He would be shown works of art that were to adorn them, made by the craftsmen under the king's patronage. Holidays, with their special ceremonies, also added a different note to the king's days and nights.

In 1837, Edmund Roberts, a "nobleman from America," as the Thai called him, was sent by Andrew Jackson on a mission to King Rama III. The ship that carried him was too large to cross the bar. A committee of noblemen met him in gold-lacquered barges, bringing him gifts of fresh food, fruits, and chests of fine tea. They carried the presents from the president to the king back with them to Bangkok. They also carried a letter to be translated and read to the king before his audience with Mr. Roberts.

The American envoy and his staff arrived at the river landing which was resplendent with tiled and gilded roofs and jutted out from the grassy, tree-lined esplanade before the palace walls. The Americans looked with amazement at the roofs and towers that soared above the palace, outlined against the turquoise sky. The crowds of people who had come to watch were held back by guards. No one was sheltered from the hot sun by a parasol for it was forbidden to raise one near the palace.

For the trip to the palace, the envoys were mounted on ponies; they were seated on flat, gold-tooled saddles. Their long American legs in the short stirrups angled upwards like those of grasshoppers. Leaving their swords at the outer gateway, they were escorted by soldiers in red-and-green uniforms. They marched past drummers each holding a drum beneath his left arm. Each drummer struck his drum a single blow with a deer's horn. Then there was a pause before the drums boomed out again. Beyond the drummers, hundreds of musicians lined the way to the audience hall.

Inside, Roberts sat on a cushion on the floor among prostrate nobles who lay as though dead. Each noble had a splendid sword, teapot, and a betel set beside him — not for use but for show. Roberts carefully arranged his feet

behind him, afraid his boots might offend the king if they projected towards him.

Gold curtains were drawn back. The nobles made another obeisance. There sat the king on his throne, an impressive sight, dressed in cloth of gold. Jewels scintillated from his high and tapering crown. The crown was made of very thin *repoussé* gold so that it might not be too heavy for the royal head.

The interview was carried on through a series of interpreters, each repeating the king's words quietly to the next, until the final one murmured the message to Roberts. The king asked some polite questions, inquiring about the health of the president, asking whether the country was flourishing and whether Roberts' voyage had been a good one. Roberts' replies were relayed back again. The king then said that he had given orders to his ministers to reply to President Jackson's letter. An official read the list of gifts the king was sending to America — there were too many to have them in the audience hall. Then the golden curtains were drawn together to show that the interview was over. The nobles rustled, rose to their feet, talking quietly together as they left the hall and had their first good look at the Americans.

The throne of the present king is an ornate chair on which he sits in European fashion, and his ministers now stand before him. Over the throne rises a ceremonial nine-storied umbrella, and on each side of the throne there is one of seven stories. The lowest story is the largest, the ones above diminishing in size. They are made of red-and-gold brocade, and at the top there is a gold finial.

This type of umbrella originated when ancient battles were fought. When a general was successful, he captured the umbrella of the opposing leader. The more umbrellas he had, the greater his power. It was more convenient in showing how many he had won to arrange them ceremonially one above the other.

Today, as it always has been, the most impressive cere-

mony in the life of a king is his coronation. There are far
too many rituals connected with it to describe them all.
Finally, after the king has placed the crown on his own
head — there is no one else sufficiently exalted to do it —
there is a magnificent procession through the city. The
present king wore a white dress uniform covered with
many orders, but formerly the king was dressed in cloth
of gold, with jeweled regalia and the high, peaked crown.

The king is carried in a splendid palanquin borne on the
shoulders of sixteen men dressed in historic military costumes dating from the time of Ayudhya. He is surrounded
by a bodyguard of noblemen. A huge, flat-domed umbrella
of red-and-gold brocade is carried over his head, and attendants shield him from the sun with fans four feet long
mounted on long handles. Bearers of spears, and nine-
tiered umbrellas march along, each in ancient costume.
Bands play gay music, drummers beat on golden drums,
accompanied by the sound of ancient trumpets and blown
conch shells. Troops of the royal guard follow, and the
army and navy line the streets, as the procession leaves
the royal temple.

The last rites for a king are also traditionally elaborate.
A year may elapse between the time of the monarch's
death and the time of his cremation. During this year, the
body, in its ceremonial urn, rests in state in the Phrasit
Throne Hall where it had been installed with many ceremonies.

Dressed in fine garments with a crown on the head and
a gold mask over the face, the body is placed in a silver urn
in a sitting posture, the knees against the chest. The urn is
forty inches high and has a sealed lid. This urn is enclosed
in an outer urn which is ten feet high and is covered with

thick plates of gold and encrusted with gems. It is eight-sided, with concave curves, rising to a crownlike peak with a spire.

Many religious rites take place during the lying in state, and it is a time of national mourning.

Hundreds of men have worked as long as four months on the funeral pyre. The pyre is made of plaster and paper mixed with glue on a wooden frame. Then it is gilded over. The materials must be new, and they are destroyed when the rites are over. The pyre is an enormous pavilion built on terraces and open on four sides. The roof rises in many tiers and is surmounted by a tall spire shaped like a Phra Chedi. All in all, it is one hundred and twenty feet tall.

The urn is carried to the pyre on a huge funeral chariot, a chariot which has carried the remains of many kings. The chariot weighs forty tons, and one hundred and sixty men holding ropes covered with red silk pull it along. Nearly as many men follow behind, dragging back on ropes. They are the chariot's brakes. The chariot has four wheels, each as tall as a man. It is carved of wood and gilded. Five curved, boat-shaped bases rise, one above the other, diminishing in size. They are carved with figures of kruts, the mythical bird, and soaring, flamelike kranok. Above is a pavilion like that on the pyre. The top is forty feet from the ground.

When the urn reaches the pyre, it is placed on a metal altar inside where the materials for the fire are laid. For hours officials and the public file past, leaving offerings of flowers and sandalwood.

The burning takes place at night. Rich brocade curtains are drawn across three sides of the pavilion; the valuable gold urn is removed and one of sandalwood substituted. The new king lights the fire in the presence of the royal relatives, and it burns throughout the night. The bones that are left are put in a small urn and are placed beside those of the king's ancestors.

Today many of the old ceremonies are gone, and there is little left of the old pageantry and pomp that made up the life of royalty. The hum of Bangkok, the honk of autos on the streets, and the tooting of ships on the river, scarcely disturb the peace of Wat Phra Keo. The gorgeously dressed court is gone, but yellow-robed monks still walk across the stone paving that, soaked with the sun, sends heat waves flickering across the same fantastic, enchanted buildings that have stood there for so long. It almost seems as if at any moment the ghost of a courtier of long ago will appear, and enter a building for a ceremony long forgotten.

17

The Thai Travel

*"Go by boat and you meet a crocodile; go by land
and you meet a tiger."*

At one time there were so few roads in Thailand that most
of the traffic was on rivers and canals. The whole country
was veined with waterways. The rivers in the mountain
valleys run between steep banks and over rapids, and are
only navigable during some seasons of the year. As they
flow southward, becoming larger and more placid, they
join the numerous rivers that drain the central plain. This
central plain is crisscrossed with thousands of canals and
channels that link the river systems in a vast network. The
mud dug from canals was once used to raise roadbeds
above flood level and for railroad embankments. Today
roads are being constructed throughout Thailand and
these, along with modern railroads and airplanes, link the
principal towns and cities.

Bangkok, which is about thirty miles from the sea, is
only five feet above sea level. Everywhere water is only a
few feet below the surface. Bangkok is higher than the
surrounding plain, raised with the earth from canals that
intersect it. At one time canals were the only means of
transportation, but now there are streets, avenues, and
roads leading out into the countryside. However, canals

are still important thoroughfares, branching out from the wide Menam Chao Phya, the largest river in Thailand.

Below the bridge that spans the river, steamers lie at wharves or are anchored to buoys in the stream. They carry flags of many nations, and bear romantic names of home ports on their sterns: Swatow, Semarang, Medan, Penang, Macao. Eddies of shrieking gulls swoop down when anything edible is thrown into the brown water. Big junks from China drop their batwing sails with a rattle as they come to a mooring.

The river pulsates with a continuous sound of motorboats. Many are towboats or ferries, but some hurry along with nothing to do but enjoy themselves. They all send out waves which set small craft and sampans bobbing.

The sampan is propelled with a flat, square-end paddle or by sculling with a long oar in the style of a Venetian gondolier. The oar is attached to an eighteen-inch wooden stanchion at the side of the boat and it takes skill to keep a straight course. The rower takes a step forward with just the right amount of twist to his body, then steps back again as he pulls against the water.

The sampans scuttle across the river, some carrying passengers. Others bear peddlers with goods to sell to the occupants of other boats or to houses along the banks. They carry market produce, tin pots and pans, or cloth and oddments — a sort of general store. Some are piled so high with red-clay jars heaped one on top of the other that one more jar would send the whole pile into the water. A vendor calls out that he has cold soda pop.

Steam launches leave a track of dark smoke as they tow a long string of empty rice boats that have brought rice down the river. A few sampans bounce along tied to the rear. The rice boats are wide and heavy, with a deep draft.

When they are laden, their gunwales are only a few inches above the slopping water. The empty ones roll along, the gunwales rising seven feet above the surface of the river. They have arched roofs made of rattan or corrugated iron that lap over one another in a series and can slide back and forth as the owner wishes. A flat roof, with removable sides so that the breeze can blow through, covers the stern. When the sides are in place, rain is kept away. These sides also form a small hut for the boatman and his family, who cook and sleep on the deck. In the shallows the boatmen strain at long poles, actually pushing the boat through the water. Sometimes the boats are propelled by matting sails if the wind and water are suitable.

Seagoing ships have one or two removable masts, each carrying one sail. The small foresail steadies the ship and helps with the steering. There are two rudders, one on each side of the sternpost. Only one is used at a time — on the side from which the wind is blowing. It takes skill to manage the boats in the Gulf, with its sand flats hidden beneath the water. Sudden storms bring treacherous, strong winds, and cold rain can hide the many rocky islands.

All Thai boats are modeled on the dugout. The small sampans are made from a hollowed-out log, which also forms the hull of all ships. The larger ones are built up above this with curved planks. There are plenty of large trees in the forests to furnish the hulls. The solid dugout is strong and will never leak, even if it strikes against snags and rocks. It is rounded at the bottom, which makes it easy to push into deep water should it stick on a sandbank.

The log is hollowed out with an adz, then soaked under water until the wood is thoroughly saturated. After forcing the sides outward to a broader shape in the middle, it is placed above a fire to dry. The planks of the hull are fastened to interior ribs, usually with wooden pegs. Waste hemp is forced into the seams for calking, then covered with a mixture of wood oil and lime. The boat is soaked with wood oil, and varnish is smeared on with cotton waste. This gives a deep reddish-brown color which gradually weathers to a grayish brown. A good boat lasts for twenty years without repairs except for a new coat of varnish or a little recalking.

Along the water front are the large sheds of the boat-builders. Wide launching runways, made of tamped-down earth, lead to the water. The smells of wood shavings and varnish fill the air, and the shed is noisy with the sounds of hammering and sawing. Below, in the water, rafts of logs float, jostled by clumps of drifting water hyacinth. A builder's wife may squat there, washing clothes.

Old boats to be repaired lie tipped against the muddy bank, and shining new ones of many sizes are attached to stakes in the water, awaiting their first owners.

Although boats of many kinds are built in Thailand, the industry was even more flourishing in the last century. At the shipyards great, seagoing junks and warships were built for the Thai navy. Trading vessels came for repairs before resuming their journeys.

The finest boats made in Thailand were the great state barges. Each was made from a single, gigantic teak tree. The high prows and sterns were carved from separate pieces of wood and added to the hull. The barges are sometimes seen on the rivers today during festivals.

Some of these boats are one hundred and fifty feet long and have a middle width of twelve feet. One of the royal barges has a figurehead twenty feet high, tapering to the head of a mythological swan. From the swan's long beak hangs a double tassel of yak's hair mounted in golden balls. Yak's hair was once thought to keep away evil spirits.

The surface of each boat is carved with designs, and covered with gold lacquer. Since the lacquer is inlaid with mosaics in pearl shell and bits of colored glass, the barges gleam as though they were made of solid gold and jewels.

In the center of the royal barge is a high, carved throne on which the king sits. It is covered by a pavilion of gilded wood hung with curtains of gold cloth and lined with scarlet silk. Seventy rowers, dressed in red garments and helmets like ancient warriors, raise their gilded oars in unison. The oars flash in the rays of the sun, water dripping like diamonds from the ends. At the stern are two steersmen, and near the bow a man stands who keeps time for the rowers, rhythmically tapping a silver spear on the deck.

During most of the year the royal barges are stored, but permission can be obtained to see them. They are kept in

an open shed on a canal, not far from the river. The barges are set on racks above shallow, muddy water which brings in flotsam with the tide. Narrow wooden boards, faded to a dim gray, form runways between the barges. They seem enormous at close view as they stretch back into the twilight of the shed. The tall, golden prows loom overhead.

The royal barges can be seen on the river when the festival of *Tod Kathin* comes in October. It is at the end of the rainy season and the period of Buddhist austerity. The king goes by water procession to take gifts to the temples: an annual offering of new robes, fans, carrying bags — anything that the monks are allowed to own. Other state barges follow, somewhat less grand, including one that carries the gifts. The spires of the palace are left behind as the barges flash and glow in the sunlight.

The people also take gifts to the monks. The river is full of boats with people in a holiday mood. The boats are decorated with streamers, flags, palm fronds, flowers, or anything else that appeals to the skill and imagination of the owner. Cheerful greetings are called across the water. Motorboats, engines throbbing, chug along towing a gay line of row boats. Bands play loudly, and radios send forth a variety of tunes. It is a carnival throughout the day.

Travel on the waterways is slow, but anyone in a hurry can reach the main towns of Thailand by airplane. There are also many thousands of miles of railroads, connected by roads and tracks, over the mountains and across dusty highlands.

Occasional autos use the rough country roads, and buses rattle along, crowded with passengers and their goods. They sit on hard benches, scattering orange and banana peels into the cloud of dust that follows.

In the wet season, many boggy roads would be impassable except to pack animals were it not for the sturdy Thai cart drawn by humped bullocks. The carts are constructed for the hard, rough work of transporting heavy loads. They can go not only on poor roads, but also on tracks partly overgrown with tall grass and weeds, and even over rice fields at the time of year when the fields are dry. Cuts in the bunds allow the wheels to pass through.

The carts have huge wheels, two yards in diameter. The rims and spokes are made of hardwood, without metal tires. The axles project outside the wheels, and a curved wooden outrigger is attached to the hubs. Wooden bars at each end support the body of the cart. This arrangement helps to distribute the weight and hold the cart steady as it lumbers along. The outriggers also hold back undergrowth so that it will not tangle in the spokes of the

The big-wheeled carts drawn by humped bullocks are a typical sight on the road to a country market place.

wheels. A woven matting roof curves over the cart, projecting gracefully at the front to protect the driver from the pounding rays of the sun. From the base of the cart, a long pole is fastened to the yoke, which fits over the bullocks' necks in front of their humps. The yoke is secured with rattan rope, which passes beneath the animals' necks.

The cart announces its coming from afar with loud shrieks and groans from the turning wheels. This does not distress the driver. The louder the sound, the more pleased he is — in fact, the maker tries to build in bigger and better squeaks. In wild country, the noise frightens away dangerous animals, and still better, will scare evil spirits that lurk along the way.

As the carter makes his way homeward in the evening, the shadows grow long and dense across the track. A bird flaps from the brush with a sudden squawk. Ahead lies a thick growth of forest, full of dark mystery. Now the friendly clamor of the cart is reassuring. As the driver nears his small village with its flickering lights and the smells of charcoal smoke and cooking curry, his family knows that he is near when they hear the individual sound of his cart.

Lighter weight carts serve rural Thai as carriages. The carts are of much the same construction as the heavier ones, but better built and not as noisy. They may be painted or decorated with lacquer. The curved roofs have openings at the sides to let in any cool breeze that might fan the passengers who sit on the floor on a thin pad.

In the towns there are three-wheeled pedicabs, called *samlors,* which have fortunately displaced the old rickshaws that were pulled by a straining man. The driver of the samlor sits on a saddle in front, working pedals, as on a bicycle. There is a seat in back onto which two passengers can crowd beneath a cotton awning.

These were once used in Bangkok, but three-wheeled motor samlors have replaced them. They speed along the streets, dodging in and out of traffic. The driver sits on a small seat at the front, his legs straddling the transmission, working the brake — and especially the accelerator. One hand is on the steering wheel, while the other squawks the horn. The streets of Bangkok are a bedlam of noise and movement, crowded with samlors, autos, bicycles, buses, and pedestrians.

In the National Museum there are carved and gilded palanquins of different periods. The early ones consisted of a thick platform like a truncated pyramid. They became more elaborate as time went on. Later ones have backs for the passengers to lean against, and side rails, and on some there are roofs overhead like those of a temple. Palanquins are mounted on two poles and are carried by bearers. Straps made of rope padded with cloth go over the bearers' shoulders to help support the weight. Ceremonial palanquins are higher, like thrones, and are borne by many bearers.

Chariots, such as were once used by royalty, are shown in wall carvings and paintings. They are depicted with front and back rising in a boat shape, the front bearing a long, thin, curving figurehead. There is a thronelike seat for the rider. The wheels are carved with designs and have an outer curved bar attached to the hub, with crossbars to support the chariot in the same type of construction as is used in carts today. In these paintings, the chariots are often drawn by mythological beasts.

In the museum there are also saddles and harnesses for ponies. The saddles are made of wood covered with leather, curving to a low pommel. Large oval leather flaps are laced to the sides with leather thongs. All are decorated with incised and colored designs. Padded straps and a cinch hold the saddle on the pony's back. The bridle is much like a modern one, but is decorated with jeweled bosses, and a tassel of yak's hair hangs from it.

Today the strong, small Thai pony is chiefly used as a pack animal or carries a rider through rough jungle or mountain tracks that are impassable to carts or trucks.

As roads become better and more numerous, bicycles and motor vehicles become more and more frequently used, and the old means of transportation are outmoded.

18

Elephants, White and Gray

*"An elephant, though it has four legs, may slip, and
no man is always right."*

Thailand and elephants are associated together. The design of the national flag used to be a white elephant on a red ground, and this emblem is still used on the naval flag.

The elephant has influenced architecture, too. There are mounting platforms the height of the elephant's back, some of them covered by roofs. Steps lead up to them, and there are carved posts beside them to which the animal was tied. Gateways in walls had to be high enough for an elephant to pass through with its tall *howdah*.

The elephant is represented in stone carvings and in paintings, walking in processions, carrying kings, and taking parts in wars. When it serves as the mount for the Brahman god, Indra, the elephant has three heads.

A white elephant, though not sacred, was very much revered. All forms of white animals were thought to contain the spirits of good and noble persons during one of their journeys through countless lives. So the white elephant, containing the soul of a great person, was thought to bring protection and prosperity to a nation that owned it. A king's favor with heaven was judged by the number of white elephants captured during his reign. The captured beasts became titled members of the nobility and lived in luxury all of their lives.

A white elephant is not really white; the Thai name for it means "albino." The skin is more or less pink, or a lighter gray than that of its common relatives, and it is adorned with pink patches. The white elephant has pale eyes surrounded by pink, and the scant hairs that grow on its body and the ends of its tail are silvery gray.

King Mongkut described a fine white elephant after its death: "The elephant's eyes were light blue surrounded by salmon color, his hair, fine, soft and white, his complexion pinkish white and his ears like silver shields. His trunk resembled a comet's tail. His footstep echoed like thunder, his expression was tender and meditative and his bearing that of an illustrious monarch."

A Thai ambassador, when he returned from England, said of Queen Victoria that he was struck by her august aspect showing descent from a race of goodly kings and rulers, that her eyes, complexion, and bearing were those of a beautiful and majestic white elephant.

This was indeed a compliment! White elephants were so much prized that when one was found, prayers and offerings were made in the temples. Nobles with a crowd of attendants served it on its triumphant journey to the capital. Paths were cut through the forest to make the way easy for its noble feet. People gathered along the way with offerings of fruit and flowers.

When the procession reached the river, a gilded barge awaited the elephant. Its quarters on board were in a carved and gilded pavilion, and it had matting woven of thin silver strips to stand upon. It was served perfumed water and the best foods were put before it on large gold and silver trays. Musicians sang and played to entertain it.

When the flotilla neared the capital, the king, with court members and crowds of Buddhist monks and Brahman priests, came to meet the elephant. They escorted the elephant to the palace, where it was installed in grand quarters.

With much ceremony, the priests read an address full of compliments. A petition was chanted to soothe and comfort the white elephant in its new estate. It was entreated not to miss the forests and mountains nor wish for its relatives. The forests were full of danger, it was told, and there it had no servants to wash and care for it. Insects would trouble it. It would drink muddy water and stones would bruise its feet. "Oh, brave and noble elephant, consent to stay in this delightful city. It has everything your heart could desire, and you are the favorite guest of his most exalted Majesty, the King," read the petition.

The title that the king bestowed upon the elephant as a noble was written on a piece of sugar cane and laid before it. If it ate the sugar cane, it signified acceptance of the honor. The elephant was endowed with lands to provide revenue for its expenses. It had his own retinue of officials and slaves.

The white elephant's stall contained a golden throne where the king sat when he came to visit the animal. In the daytime the elephant was bound by ropes covered with scarlet silk to carved upright posts. This was to refrain the elephant from expressing any dissatisfaction with all the pomp by attacking admiring visitors. It was allowed to be free at night.

During state ceremonies the white elephant's place was beside the palace gate; dressed in fine regalia, it added dignity and honor to the occasion. Its tusks were circled with heavy, wrought-gold bands set with jewels; it wore a necklace and a gold headpiece, and a silken cloth with gold fringe. Its counterpart is seen in old carvings on stone walls and in paintings.

Through the centuries the white elephant's grand state has gradually diminished. When one was found during the present king's reign, it was considered a fortunate event, but the court did not have to go to meet the elephant. When it was brought to Bangkok, the king gave it a title and the traditional regalia, but with very little pomp. Its stall has become a simple affair more suited to its needs. It is in a large enclosure at the zoo, where it leads a much freer and happier life than did its predecessors.

All wild elephants were once considered the king's property. At one time so many elephants were used in war and for heavy labor, there were periodic elephant roundups attended by the king and his court. These were more exciting than a rodeo. The last roundup was during the early part of this century.

A large elephant stockade still stands near the old summer capital of Lopburi. It is made of strong double walls of large teak logs partly buried in the earth to withstand the force of the huge, hurtling bodies. The space between the stakes is wide enough to allow a man to slip through, but too narrow for an elephant. The logs are carved at the tops like the hitching posts of Venetian gondolas.

At the roundup, the king and court sat on a platform at one side of the stockade. The king sat under his many-storied umbrella, surrounded by attendants. The villagers climbed trees or found other vantage points from which they watched the show.

When a herd of wild elephants was sighted, tame female elephants were taken into the forest to lure the wild

animals back to the stockade through a funnel-shaped entrance. Then huge logs were dropped across the opening
behind them.

Tame elephants lined up between the frightened, dangerous herd and the onlookers.

Experts judged the captured elephants and selected the
best. The color of the animal had to be good. It should not
have broken tusks, for tusks were necessary for work as
well as appearance. An elephant's tail had to be intact, too.
Often part of the tail had been bitten off in a fight. The
captors risked death, darting in and out amongst the in-
furiated herd. They prodded and drove the selected animals until the elephants were tired. Then the elephants
were driven into a smaller enclosure at the side of the

main stockade. After many tries, a man managed to slip a loop of strong rattan rope around one elephant's foot. The end of the rope was seized by assistants who made it fast to a heavy post.

When the best of the elephants had been corralled, the rest of the herd was allowed to escape.

The captured elephants were left alone for several days without food. Then they were untied and joined by tame elephants. They were given water and food, and in a surprisingly short time — a few months — they were tamed.

Wild elephants travel in herds through the forests and jungles and are found in most parts of Thailand except the plains, where it is too hot for them. In 1951, when the number of herds was found to be decreasing, they were put under strict government control.

Wild elephants do not usually attack a man unless frightened or molested, but the countrypeople fear them. Farmers are forbidden to kill them, although roving bands sometimes descend on the small farms near the forests and raid the crops disastrously. Elephants especially love wide, succulent banana leaves and may leave a whole grove trampled underfoot.

How horrifying for a farmer's family to wake in the night to the scrunch of falling banana trees, the thump of many huge feet, loud gruntings, and the sound of the elephants whistling through their trunks with satisfaction as they gorge. Or there may be an occasional loud, angry trumpeting as two of the beasts strive for the same tidbit.

As the farmer peers out at the great shapes looming in the darkness, he wonders if the menacing monsters will push over his frail house. Huddling with his family, he reminds the house spirit of the food and flowers they have provided for it, and the stick of incense when a little money had been saved. Will the spirit graciously come to the rescue before the marauding gang finds the store of rice? Or will the family and the spirit have to go hungry through the winter?

The elephant is still a useful worker. An adult wild elephant can be trained for work in a few months. For a year or two he is not given much work to do. During that time he adjusts to his new life; for a long time he feels the strain of his captivity. But once trained, the bull elephant can work until he is fifty or sixty years old. He is intelligent, willing, and obedient.

When a baby is born to one of the working females, it follows its mother about until it is five years old. Then it becomes independent. At fourteen it is trained for light work.

Each elephant keeps the same driver for a lifetime. In spite of its size, an elephant panics easily at unusual sights and sounds. The driver believes that when he is riding his beast, the elephant knows it has two hearts and has not been left alone to face danger. When an elephant is hungry, it lets its driver know by grunting and striking the ground with its trunk.

The elephant is used for journeys in rough country where there are no trails or railroads. It is a slow way to travel. Long stops must be made so that the elephant may eat the large quantities of food it requires. The elephant can average five miles an hour, according to the nature of the country. It appears to be shambling along, but a walking man must hurry to keep up.

The elephant makes its way through the forests, breaking branches and small trees from its path, pushing through tangled vines. It is helped by its driver who hacks at the growth with a long knife. The elephant can descend deep ravines, half sitting and sliding. When it crosses a river, it measures the depth with its trunk. In deep water, it holds its trunk above its head so it can breathe, its back a safe island for the riders.

Riding an elephant is not a comfortable affair, but the Thai say one becomes used to the motion. The elephant's back slopes downward towards each leg as it is raised. As the elephant walks, the carrier platform sways in what seems to be a precarious manner.

The platform is part of a howdah and is supported by curved wooden braces like a saddle which fit over the elephant's back. There is a low railing about a foot high at the sides and back. A curved, woven basket-roof keeps off the hot sun and rain. The whole contraption is set on a pad and held on the animal's back by bands around his stout middle, under his neck, and beneath his tail. Passengers sit with their feet on the elephant's neck, or curled up on the flat platform. The driver sits just behind the elephant's head, his legs hanging down behind the animal's flapping ears. The driver carries a goad, a blade with a curved tip set at right angles to a handle.

The howdah has not changed its shape through the centuries. It is shown in Thai art and there are many howdahs in the National Museum that were used by nobles and abbots. These howdahs are elaborately decorated. Some are made entirely of ivory, except for the hood. They are warm and golden with the patina of age. They have bands of ornament and carved spindles and rails. Others are of carved and gilded wood, with hoods covered with designs in gold and black lacquer, and lined with red. The floors are of woven cane with enough spring for comfort.

There is a special howdah for a war elephant. It has a small cannon mounted in the center to shoot over the animal's head. War elephants were very carefully trained so they would not be stampeded by loud bangs and bursts of powder.

A leader, when he rode an elephant to battle, sat on its neck on a pad with cloth-covered ropes to hold it in place. On the howdah above, a many-storied umbrella proclaimed the leader's rank. An assistant sat behind, ready to hand him any of the many weapons in the racks at the sides. The assistant also held bunches of peacock feathers in each hand, to signal the leader's orders to his followers. Another man, who sat on a pad at the back, carried the goad and guided the elephant.

There are old elephant bells at the museum. They are the same kind as are hung from the necks of elephants today. Made of metal and about a foot high, the bells look rather like sleigh bells with ridges around them. They are cast in two pieces and have a metal ball inside. Each driver knows the distinctive sound of his elephant's bell. At a camp during the night, the bells jangle as the animals feed. The animals are allowed to wander freely, only partially fettered with loose ropes tied between their forelegs. The sounds of the bells help the drivers find their elephants in the morning.

As well as serving as transport animals, elephants work in the lumber camps of the great teak forests. They used to help load logs at ports, but modern machinery has replaced them.

Trained elephants are very valuable property. A supervisor who works for a lumber company must be able to care for the animals' health and know how to treat their injuries. The supervisor travels from one lumber camp to another. When the sun is low and the day's work done, the elephants are paraded before him. He watches them for lameness. The drivers tell their big charges to kneel. The supervisor looks the animals over for abrasions from their harnesses; he examines their feet for cuts or thorns; he inspects their eyes. If one of the elephants is ill, it may be dosed with medicine or taken from work for a while.

The Thai logging industry could not get along without the aid of trained elephants. Machinery would be useless in this roadless, rough country with rugged mountain gorges down which torrents rush in the rainy season.

The mainstay of Thailand's logging industry is teak-wood, one of the world's most valuable woods. It is hard, resists rot and termites, does not split, and has a fine appearance. The timber is not only used extensively in Thailand, but also is exported to all parts of the world.

Teak trees do not grow in large stands, but are scattered through the forests in the northern part of Thailand. There the climate and soil conditions are suitable. The teak trees can reach an age of three hundred years. Some of the large trees are one hundred and fifty feet high and nine feet in diameter, although many of the largest were cut long ago.

There are government forestry officers who supervise the teak industry and guard against indiscriminate cutting. The trees that may be felled are marked with a blaze. Part of the teak area is reserved for reforestation, allowing the young, small trees to age and grow. The forestry officer is always on the watch for fire. Fire destroys the undergrowth and with it the young teak and seedlings. Besides fire, the young trees are sometimes damaged by storms or herds of wild elephants.

The trees that have been designated by the forestry

officer are killed by girdling — cutting deeply around the base of the tree. The wood must be dry, so the logs will float down the river to the sawmills. Green and sappy wood is too heavy and will sink.

Long leaves droop like yellow rags on the dead trees, or look like sleeping huddles of yellow-brown bats. The trees stand until the rainy season. The ground is then soft enough so that the timber will not break as it crashes to the ground. The woodsmen cut away the branches and bark, and then cut two square holes in one end.

Now the elephant begins its logging work. It must drag the log across the ground to the nearest stream. Chains passed through the logs are attached to the elephant's working saddle. This saddle, made of wood, consists of crosspieces at each end joined together by crossbars. The saddle is lined with soft bark, or it rests on a pad made of bark, or it is stuffed with tree cotton, called kapok. The pad protects the elephant's back as it tugs at the heavy log which may weigh two tons. A breastband crossing the elephant's chest is fastened to the chains. This must fit each individual animal exactly, and is usually made of bark rope by the elephant's driver. The rope is soaked with fat to protect the animal's hide.

At the time the trees are felled, the rains are not yet heavy. Only a little water runs in the middle of the stream beds where the elephants have hauled the logs. They shove and push the timber into place, lifting it with their tusks, their trunks curled above to balance a log as they stack it. There the teak awaits the heavy monsoon rains.

For days big towering clouds pile up at the horizon. At night they block out the stars that shone so brilliantly for months. An hour or so of rain falls each day; then the hard, bright sun comes out again.

One day the rain bursts down from the dark sky. It can be heard roaring across the forest as it approaches. Sheets of water fall day after day, and heavy mist fills the valleys. The workers are always wet, even their pay must be sent in silver, for paper money would disintegrate.

The rivers flood; the swirling water lifts the teak. The twisting logs bang and crash, whacking each other as they hurtle down the rivers on their long journey to the sawmills. Not even an elephant could go into the torrent.

But toward the end of the rainy season, when the water has ebbed, the drivers take their elephants into the water to push stranded logs into the slowing river and take advantage of the last of the current. The intelligent animals know just which log to move to break up a jam.

The teak floats down past rapids, until it leaves the mountain streams and reaches the quiet waters of the larger rivers. Here the logs are measured at government stations and a tax collected according to size. Each log is easily identified by the logging company's mark it bears.

Then the logs are made up into large rafts of two to four hundred logs each. Several men, often with their families, take charge of a raft, living in a small thatched hut built on board. They drift down river through the long, hot, lazy days. They push with long poles to keep the raft in the current, and try to avoid sandbanks or patches of floating, tangled water hyacinths as large as islands. At night they tie up at the riverbank. They stop at small villages, where they buy fresh food, bargaining about the price with much entertaining argument, and talk over the latest news. It takes months to reach Bangkok. It is estimated that three years elapse from the time a tree is felled until it comes to the end of its journey.

Near Bangkok, the rafts are packed together, tied to

*At the sawmill, teakwood, the mainstay of Thailand's
logging industry, will be sorted, graded, and stacked.*

stakes, where they wait to go to the sawmills. After the
quiet days, how exciting the busy river must seem to the
lumbermen. Full of traffic and boats of all sorts, the river
is lined with houses and factories on its banks.

When they reach the mills, the largest and best logs are
squared. Others are cut into planks, and small pieces are
cut into shingles and strips for parquet flooring. The sawmills do as little sawing as possible, for each cut loses
about half-an-inch in sawdust. But the sawdust is not
wasted. It is used as fuel for the machinery.

Teak is exported all over the world and it is much prized
for shipbuilding, decking, homes, and fine furniture. Japan

buys teak with particularly beautiful grain for use in her crafts. This grain is called "flowered" grain and brings a premium price.

The less choice grades are sold to India, China, and also used in Thailand. The Thai use it for constructing buildings, boats, carts, and furniture.

Teak was once the monopoly of kings and nobles, and was used in palaces and temples. The big timbers which support temple roofs are made of teak, as are the carved ends of gables. The large temple doors and window shutters are made of huge single slabs.

Many beautiful things remain from the past because of the durability of teak. There are carved thrones and palanquins and funeral chariots used in royal ceremonies.

Today teak is used by anyone who can afford it. Small carved models of polished teak are made for the tourist trade and sold in Bangkok shops. They represent both mythical figures and everyday things such as carts, boats, and plowmen with buffaloes. There are enough elephants to form innumerable herds. Many are small, but some stand three feet high and have real ivory tusks.

Ivory has always been valuable and there are criminals who cut off an elephant's tusks for the ivory. Figurines, small boxes, and jewelry are made of it. Gongs hang suspended between two tusks mounted on bases of silver or ebony. In the National Museum there are many especially fine tusks, either highly polished or intricately carved, which were mounted and used as ornaments. They were selected for their beautiful curves, and some are eight feet tall.

Although elephants are no longer seen in the streets of Bangkok, there are plenty of teak or ivory reminders of them in the shops. The carver often represents the ele-

phants dragging teak logs, appropriately showing part of
their work. And appropriately enough, it is the teak in the
hands of the craftsman which will bring a model of an
elephant to the home of the Thai. So that elephants and
teak, and Thai are all linked together.

19

The Bountiful Soil

*"Trees and plants are the children of the earth,
produced by the sun and the rain."*

The countryside and the forests of Thailand supply many useful trees and plants, either cultivated or growing wild. Their products are used in the home, in crafts, for commerce, or for export.

The forest trees furnish dyes, gums, and oils as well as lumber and firewood. The wharves at the ports are piled high with forest products. The products make their way into every Thai home. The lumber is used for furniture. A large slab, cut across the trunk of a tree, is mounted on legs and forms a table. It is left irregular in shape, and the grain shines through a high polish.

Rubber used to be collected from several species of wild forest trees, but now it is mostly cultivated commercially on plantations. The small collector sells the sap as it comes in the form of latex from cuts in the trees' bark. Bigger growers process their rubber, making large sheets for export or domestic use. Thailand manufactures bicycle tubes and tires, rubber shoes and soles, and ebonite, which is a hard rubber.

Another important export of Thailand is a resinous oil obtained from a forest tree called *Yang*, and this is also the name of the oil. Yang makes a fine varnish that is affected by neither water nor sunlight. Boats are made watertight with this varnish. It is used as an undercoat on objects to be gilded, and holds gold leaf firmly to the surface. Waterproof umbrellas, made of paper stretched on a bamboo frame, are covered with the varnish. When it rains, these umbrellas, golden brown and shining, appear like mushrooms in the streets. Varnished paper lanterns, which open like two umbrellas joined at the rims, hang in doorways and in front of shops. Painted with black or red lettering, they announce what goods are sold within.

The Yang tree is one of the largest of the wild forest trees, and it may rise one hundred and twenty-five feet before the branches begin. The oil drips into big, open holes that are cut into the trunk, and is dipped out and placed in a large section of bamboo. When the flow of oil ceases, a fire is built in the basin-shaped hole and this causes the oil to drip again. The thick sap, a dirty white, is strained through a cloth; first it turns brown, then black. It is stored in jars, with a layer of water on top to keep the air away, for contact with the air would harden the oil.

Before the coming of kerosene and electricity, this oil was burned to give light. Torches are still made of it and are used in some country districts today. Small torches are used to light charcoal fires. To make torches, oil is poured into a hole in the ground and rotted wood added. The substance is kneaded into a thick paste and a portion of the paste is wrapped in large leaves, or in bark, and bound with narrow strips of rattan. Lighted, the torches flame at the top, giving a smoky, flaring light. When a man carries one along a pathway at night, his great black shadow staggers along behind him like a drunken giant. Every shadow of a tree or bush seems to be a moving form that sneaks along, following him stealthily, or ready to spring and meet him. What a safe thing a kerosene lantern or a flashlight would seem to be!

The shining lacquer coating that covers so many things in the Orient is made from this same resinous tree oil. Thai craftsmen cover small tables with lacquer, as well as bowls, trays, cups, vases, and boxes of many sorts. Some boxes are cylindrical with a tray inside, and have covers with deep sides that fit entirely over them. The surface is durable and ornamental. Sometimes the base is made of wood; sometimes it is tightly-woven split bamboo.

A coating of the black oil is smeared on the foundation with a flat stick that slants at the end. At this stage the surface is fairly rough. The object is set aside to dry and harden for twenty-four hours. Then it is polished, another coat added, and then repolished.

A design may now be painted on the lacquered surface with some of the resin mixed with different colors of fired clay ground to a very fine powder. The mixture is brown, tan, or light gray, or coloring matter may be added.

A pattern can also be engraved in the lacquer surface with a style. Then it is painted over with color or gold and polished until the paint wears away from the higher part of the pattern. The color is left only in the incisions.

Sometimes mother-of-pearl is cut in small pieces and these are set elaborately into the lacquer while it is still soft. More lacquer is added to the spaces between the shell. When dry, the surface is ground down to a smooth finish on a lathe. Many objects are decorated in this

This detail is from a temple door at a Bangkok wat.
The door is black lacquer inlaid with mother-of-pearl.

fashion. Bowls with pointed covers stand in a tray on an elaborate pedestal, holding gifts that are taken to the temple. Old Thai books have covers with the pearl-shell designs. This type of decoration is also used on the shutters of windows and the doors of temples.

In each type of work, the object is given a final coat of thin lacquer-resin, then polished for the last time. To make the polish, two scraps of fired clay, wet with water, are rubbed together until they are ground to a fine powder. This is mixed with water to form a paste which is smeared onto the lacquered surface. Another clay shard is used to rub the surface of the object until it is shiny and gleaming.

The resinous tree-oil, which is the base of the lacquer, is not the same substance as lac, which is supplied by scale insects and furnishes varnishes and dyes. Thousands of these insects lay their eggs on the twigs of many varieties

A woman produces lacquer in the traditional manner —
straining the resinous sap of a tree through a cloth.

of trees. There are so many insects, and they multiply so quickly, that their name was taken from the Sanskrit word *lakh* which means "one hundred thousand."

When the larvae hatch from the eggs, they suck sap and incase themselves in a crust an inch thick that covers the whole twig. The twigs are gathered and pulverized, then heated in water to dissolve the scaly substance and the dye. The water is strained from the resinous material and allowed to evaporate. The residue is molded in cakes. Artist's colors, called *lakes*, are made from the lac. The hues are beautiful roses, reds, and browns. Lac dye is a very ancient industry, but its value declined when chemical dyes appeared on the market.

The soft mass of resinous material is repeatedly washed and dried; then it is placed in cloth bags near the heat of a fire. A worker twists the bag as an American cook twists a bag of fruit to make jelly. The melted resin drips out and forms small flakes as it dries. The flakes look like little shells, and the flaky substance is called shellac. It is made into commercial shellac by mixing it with a solvent. Thousands of tons are exported from Thailand each year to be turned into shellac, sealing wax, and phonograph records.

Charcoal is used to make the hot fires for these industries and many others. Its pungent smoke drifts all over Thailand from innumerable cooking stoves.

The best grade of charcoal comes from the mangrove trees that grow in muddy, tidal swamps. These swamps are the most impenetrable of Thailand's jungles, accessible only from waterways. Snaky, stiltlike roots hold the mangroves above the water. They grow rapidly, holding back silt which forms new marshlands. Endless shallow lanes of water twist about, each looking like the other. If the workers were not familiar with the district, they would soon be lost in the scary stillness.

The tall, shiny green foliage seems to open before a boat, lead it on, then quickly close behind as the track curves. In the heat of the day even birdcalls are stilled. An occasional white heron plops down in the water for a fish or a snake. The knobby eyes of a crocodile, half hidden in the brackish water, stare malignantly.

After working all day felling the mangrove trees, the workmen hurry with their loaded boats to the lumber camps. They leave the swamps before the dusk descends quickly and brings with it swarms of fierce, stinging mosquitoes.

At the camps the logs are sawn into firewood lengths, and the bark saved for dyes and for tanning. The wood is burned in brick kilns to make the charcoal.

Women fan the charcoal cooking fires with rattan fans. Strong, flexible rattan is woven into mats and baskets of many shapes and sizes that are used in industry, and to hold almost anything. Rattan is woven and twisted over bamboo frames, to form chairs and tables.

Many species of the rattan vine twists about the forest trees throughout Thailand. It grows in a variety of thicknesses and some of the vines are six hundred feet in length. It has sharp thorns, and laces back and forth, forming a formidable barrier. Collecting the resistant rattan is a hard job. Here, again, the elephant often helps — he is protected by his thick hide.

As forests recede before civilization, palms spring up on the edges of cleared jungles. One of the most useful palms is the coconut. Coconut palms, both wild and cultivated, grow along rivers in groves, and in home gardens. Their great, spreading fronds nearly meet over narrow canals. Small houses in their shade may be thatched with their long leaves. The palms grow rapidly and may live to be over one hundred years old.

At the base of the fronds, the nuts, covered by a thick husk, grow on branching stems. Inside the fibrous husk there is a hard-shelled nut which contains a layer of "meat," soft when the nut is green and hard when it is brown and ripe. The hollow inside is filled with a sweet liquid that is pleasant and refreshing to drink. The Thai use both the liquid and the meat of coconuts, both green and ripe, in cooking many different dishes — sweet dishes as well as tart ones.

The nut is split open and dried in the sun or over a smoky fire to make commercial copra. Oil is pressed from the nut and is used for cooking; girls smooth it into their hair to keep the hair sleek and shining. After the oil is extracted, the meat is fed to cattle as fodder.

In the quiet season after the rice harvest, a farmer's wife may strip the side leaves from the long stems of the coconut fronds to make fans and to weave mats, baskets, or hats. Hats shaped like lamp shades are worn by women when they work in the sun. These are woven over a hat shaped, wooden block which is mounted solidly on a low stand. Inside the hat, to hold it on the head, there is a rounded rack of rattan. These hats are seen everywhere, on boat and marketwomen, and those working in the fields.

A small girl's clever fingers can twist and weave the leaves into toys, small boats, or planes, and into animals or fish which sometimes hang in groups over the baby's cradle, like mobiles.

The fiber from around the nut is springy and water resistant. It is called *coir*. Many Americans have mats of coir outside their doors on which they wipe their shoes. Coir is used in cordage, fish nets, for insulation, and to make fenders to keep boats from rubbing against a wharf.

A piece of coconut husk is used as a scrubbing brush in Thai houses. Half a coconut shell is made into a dipper or a bowl. The half shell was once a measure of capacity, before the Thai standardized their measures to the metric system. What heated arguments there must have been between buyers and sellers, the merchant measuring with a small shell and the buyer bringing his own, a fine big one!

The Thai make many useful things from palm leaves.
Here an elephant driver fashions a palm-leaf umbrella.

The areca palm rises straight and slender above the massive coconut palm. Its short fronds turn back in graceful curves above stems that bear the nuts enclosed in an orange husk. The chief product is the nuts. They furnish dye and are used in tanning. The areca palm was greatly prized for this nut when nearly all the Thais chewed betel. The habit of chewing betel is declining fast, although many of the older people in country districts still chew betel as a stimulant.

Betel sets contained this nut, other substances for chewing, and the implements with which to prepare them. There was a pair of scissors, something like garden clippers, for cutting fresh areca nuts into small pieces; a mortar to grind the hard, dried ones. The hot, aromatic betel leaves are packed in a flattened, metal cornucopia; powdered lime, tobacco, and the bark from a tree which contains red dye, all part of the mixture, are kept in small boxes. A box of lip pomade concludes the list of paraphernalia. The sets were often very beautiful, made of gold, silver, or lacquer, covered with designs and inlaid with gems. Some fine old ones are in the museum at Bangkok. A valuable set gave a person prestige. When a rich noblewoman went out for a visit, she was followed by a row of attendant girls. One carried a teapot; one a fan; one a tray with small porcelain drinking bowls with shallow, domed covers; and one carried a betel set.

When betel is chewed, it forms a red liquid in the mouth which the chewer constantly spits out. At one time every house had a decorative jar for this. Out of doors the squatting chewer was surrounded by a circle of red stains on the ground that looked like blood.

The mouth and gums of the chewer were stained a bright red, and the teeth gradually became an enameled black, a sign of beauty at one time. The betel tray contained a pot of black substance to touch up any spots on the teeth from which the surface may have rubbed off. Today white teeth are admired and are cleaned after an occasional chew. Few young people chew betel at all.

More important than the palms in Thai economy is bamboo. The Thai could scarcely get along without bamboo, they use it for so many things. It grows quickly all about the country, an inexhaustible supply. It is not a tree but a giant member of the grass family. It has hollow, round stems of different thicknesses, the largest three feet around. They grow in joints separated inside by flat, woody membranes. In some species the membranes are near together, in others, six feet apart. There are many varieties, some no higher than a man, and others as high as one hundred feet.

The thick clumps are made up of canes massed in a tough tangle of stalks and cross branches. Suckers reach out in every direction to form new shoots. When the shoots are about a foot high they are tender and juicy, and when boiled they make a tasty vegetable.

Its narrow leaves fluttering in the slightest breeze, bamboo spreads along roads and waterways, and on bunds and higher ground in the rice fields. At the edge of the jungles, the grassy glades among the thickets are the haunts of peacock and orange and green jungle fowl, their nests in the dense clumps are safe from marauders.

Many small houses are constructed on bamboo frames. Scaffolding made of the canes is strong and flexible, and can be adapted to fit any surface. Unlike metal, bamboo does not expand in the hot sun. Fishing poles, stakes, and weirs are made of bamboo, also the masts and spars of small ships.

Tobacco and dyed cloth dry on bamboo frames. When a woman washes the family's clothes, she hangs them to dry on a bamboo pole, or thrusts a pole through the sleeves of shirts and blouses so the clothes will dry comparatively free from wrinkles.

In Thai kitchens, liquids are often kept in large bamboo segments; food is also cooked in the segments. Cups are made from smaller sections of bamboo. Bamboo even takes the place of cans in Thai industry, holding gums or sugar sirup.

Many layers of bamboo are bound together to form rafts for carrying loads down the rivers. These rafts are unsinkable, for their natural watertight compartments are full of air. Rafts of bamboo stalks float to paper factories where they are ground into pulp and made into paper by modern

machinery. Thailand has a plentiful supply of bamboo which is turned into quality writing paper, wrapping paper, and newsprint.

When split with a wedge-shaped knife, the bamboo strips can be woven into mats for sleeping or sitting. Smaller mats are made into baskets or table mats for exporting. Some of the bamboo baskets are swung on the ends of bamboo poles and carried across the shoulders. The baskets hold portable kitchens, or are filled with fruits, vegetables, or even baby ducks. The loads jounce up and down as the bearer trots along; the flexible bamboo pole bounces and bends with each step. Loads of firewood or fodder, bales of cloth, clay jars, discarded kerosene tins filled with water — almost anything can be carried this way. (Twigs of green leaves are placed on top of the water. The leaves keep the water from sloshing over with the swinging, jouncing motion.)

The Thai have a word — *hap* — which means the carrying of weights across the shoulders on a stick. It has come to mean the amount a man can carry this way: a man's load, or a weight of 133 pounds.

Stools, benches, and furniture are made of bamboo. Some of the furniture is in Western designs and is exported for world trade. The making of furniture is taught now in the crafts schools.

A long list of bamboo products — but only a partial one! Like the numbers of other products that come from the trees and plants that grow in Thailand's rich, fertile soil, the list seems inexhaustible.

20

Beauty From Mud

"The lotus, growing in the mud, aspires to the sky."

Mud is one of the easiest of materials to obtain. From prehistoric times, and in every country, man has used mud for many purposes. Cut in blocks and dried in the sun, it is used to build walls and houses. It is baked into brick. Washed and kneaded, clay, often mixed with other materials, is formed into utensils, pottery, figures, and architectural decorations.

Votive tablets made of clay, dating from as early as the seventh century, are found by the thousands around Thailand, in caves and ruins of monuments. These tablets are small plaques, three to ten inches tall. They are squared at the base and arched or rounded at the top. They carry religious symbols in relief. The Thai call them "sacred imprints." They were made from a piece of clay pressed while damp between two copper plates on which the design was deeply indented. The clay was then dried but not fired.

Some of the early designs seem to indicate that these tablets were mementos brought back from Buddhist shrines in India, in the same way that medals are brought back by pilgrims from sacred shrines in Europe. The imprint of a bo tree symbolizes the place where Buddha attained omniscience as he sat meditating under this tree. He first preached the law in a deer park near Benares. This was called "revolving the wheel of the law," so tablets commemorating this event carry the design of a wheel supported by two deer. There are many more designs on the tablets which were inspired by the life of Buddha.

Starting as objects of remembrance, the plaques soon became objects of reverence. It became an act of merit to make them, as it was meritorious to make statues of Buddha. The clay tablets could be pressed out easily by a pious person who had no skill or wealth. He could rent a press for a few small coins, possibly in the courtyard of a temple. The finished tablets could be placed among the flowers and incense at the altar, or carried home as a reminder of the sacred law.

Early remains of pottery are found in Thailand — crude, unglazed earthenware made for everyday use. Only the upper classes used vessels of silver or bronze. Later, in the thirteenth century, glazed stoneware was made. In some, the glaze was only applied at the top and allowed to run down in streaky patterns.

There are very few unbroken specimens of old Thai pottery and they are highly prized. Fragments have been found among ancient ruins and at the sites of old kilns. These are mostly near the towns of Sukhodaya and Swankalok. Here the best ceramics were made during a short period from the early fourteenth century to about the middle of the fifteenth century.

Outside the towns, along the river, are the remains of the old kilns, once described as resembling the shells of turtles. They have now crumbled into mounds, burying shards with earth. Weeds and tangled growth cover the discards thrown out by many generations of potters. Some of the discards have fused together into strange, beautiful forms, that look like modernistic sculpture. The earth has been dug over many times in the search for something valuable now that the pottery is of historical interest and has a sales value.

At times a farmer may turn up an old pot or shard with his plow. It is strange, and he fears it may contain a malign spirit that will harm him. He may hurriedly rebury it, or, more bravely, carry it to the wat, for any evil would surely be exorcised in such holy surroundings. In this way, the monks have been able to preserve pieces of historic interest.

The king who ruled Sukhodaya in the fourteenth century sent missions to China bearing gifts. The emissaries were impressed by the fine ceramics that were made there and brought back a group of potters with them, introducing Chinese techniques to Sukhodaya.

At first the designs were strongly influenced by the Chinese, but soon they became typically Thai. Some of the patterns have borders of lines or dots, surrounding conventional fish or animals. There are lotus designs and other floral motives. These are painted in a dark color on a light ground, sometimes in a darker value of the tinted glaze. The beauty of the pottery is chiefly due to its fine forms.

Elaborate, glazed architectural ornaments were also made at Sukhodaya; tiles for roofs, decorations for gable ends and finials, and mythical figures and demons. But the clay found near Sukhodaya was of inferior quality. After about twenty years the potters moved northward to Swankalok where better materials could be found — good clays that fired into a hard body. Pottery was no longer made at the old site, but quantities of tiles and ornaments were still made there.

Celadon ware, made in China, was in demand throughout the Orient. It was thought that this porcelain would crack or change color if the celadon vessel contained poison — a useful property in the opinion of the rulers and leaders who feared for their lives. Also, medicine prepared in a celadon vessel was supposed to have superior curative powers. Sometimes a fine piece of celadon ware was ground to powder to form a medicinal ingredient.

At Swankalok, the potters made ceramics resembling celadon for the export trade. It was very similar to the Chinese-made ware, but technically inferior. It had incised designs and a greenish-gray glaze. Swankalok celadon has been found in Java, the Philippines, Japan, and

A roof tile in the form of a dragon. It has a cream-colored glaze, incised decorations, manganese details.

even as far away as Egypt. The Japanese admired it for its
fine shapes and subdued colors, and used it in their tea
ceremonies. Many pieces have been preserved in Japan,
more so than are found in Thailand, where it was not especially valued until lately.

The kilns were two hundred and fifty miles from the
sea. It was a long, slow journey to the ports. The ceramics
were piled on river boats. Then yellow matting sails were
spread to catch the breeze. The boats were laboriously
poled along when the breeze failed. Finally, the ceramic
boats reached the main river and ports on the Gulf of Siam.
The pottery was then probably transferred to the backs of
elephants who trekked through the forest to western ports.

At Swankalok, ceramic dolls a few inches long were
made for little Thai girls. The dolls resembled members of
the court. Often their garments were painted on, but
sometimes the dolls were dressed in real cloth. There were
also small animal and human figurines — probably used
for votive offerings and for sorcery rites.

Many small images of this period have been found. One
represents a mother sitting on the floor and holding her
baby. In each case, the mother's head has been broken off.
Whenever a new baby was born, one of these broken-
headed figures was put outside the door of the house. This
was believed to ward off evil spirits. Because the spirits
were stupid, they believed that the mother figurine was
the real mother and was dead, so it would be useless to
bother her further.

In the last half of the fifteenth century, during wars
between the Thai states, the potteries at Swankalok were
abandoned. (Old kilns, with unfinished contents still waiting to be fired, have been discovered there.) The northern
state of Chiengmai captured the craftsmen. The captive

*An example of 14th century Thai pottery work, this head
of a giant is grey-brown with a beautiful celadon glaze.*

potters carried on in a small way, but the foreign trade in
fine ceramics was left to China.

After the decline of the Thai potteries, the kings and
nobles ordered porcelain made for them in China from
Thai designs. These pieces were typically Thai in shape
as well as in ornament. The ware was highly decorated in
many colors and with gold, all under a transparent glaze.
Some have overall patterns of flowers or flowing, geometrical designs. Sometimes the patterns are backgrounds
for a mythical animal design. The vessels shine like shot
silk, or the sheen on a pigeon's breast.

Not all the Chinese ware was decorated in China, however. There were times when the porcelain was brought

from China to be decorated by Thai workmen. And in Thailand, some of the Chinese porcelain teapots were fitted with metal handles and rims.

Some very valuable teapots were made in Thailand of hard rock ground to powder and treated like clay. After firing, the surface was polished with a file coated with an abrasive mixture of sticlac and ground sapphire. It left a slight coating on the pot. Next, the surface of the pot was polished with the hard, smooth outer surface of a strip of bamboo. This process took weeks to accomplish. Finally the teapot was sleek and shining as though it had been glazed. The color might be brown, reddish, or purple-gray.

At the University of Fine Arts in Bangkok, students of ceramics are taught modern techniques as well as those of the old Thai potters.

There is a factory that turns out copies of Swankalok celadon ware. Many of the things are in the old shapes: Naga heads, mythological figures, elephants, and other animals. Some of these are lamp bases intended for the Western trade. Modern dinnerware is manufactured as are ashtrays and casserole dishes — all of the same materials that were used so long ago.

Utility ware is still made as it has been for centuries. Here are the huge water jars looking as if they still stood on a sailing ship, carrying the crew's water for long voyages, or used as containers for oil, honey, or sugar. They are know in the Orient as "Siam jars." In Thailand, these jars stand in rows below the house eaves to catch rainwater for the dry season. They hold bath water in the houses. And smaller, similar jars stand on shelves as containers for money or odds and ends.

Sometimes a cooking pot is placed on its side before a

house, with a fierce face drawn on the bottom, scowling dangerously. It wards off the spirit of illness.

Along country roads, kindly householders put out smaller jars of water with a dipper so that thirsty passers-by may drink. These jars are often placed on a wooden stand with a thatched roof over them to keep the water cool, shaded from the sun.

Since larger industries are not allowed in the main city of Bangkok, the potters' sheds are built along the river and canal banks, across the water from the city. Heaps of pots and jars are stacked on front of the sheds, waiting to be taken by boat to the city. They form a wall of soft oranges, browns, and reds. The colors of the pots and jars indicate the way in which the clay responded to the firing. Boats lie at the bank piled high with water jars and rosy cooking pots that will soon be stained with soot from charcoal fires. There are large and small stoves shaped like flowerpots and glazed teapots. Above, on the bank, broken pottery and shards lie scattered about on the ground which is covered with a reddish dust and masses of clay. There are piles of brown bamboo baskets and heaps of straw for packing small articles, and clay is everywhere — in piles, lumps, and smears, on tools, and on workmen.

Heaps of clay, dug from riverbanks and fields, are soaked with water from the canal. Then workmen trample it thoroughly with their bare feet. They feel hard lumps or stones and pick them out. When clay is needed at the shed, a piece is cut off with a wire that is strung across a wooden bow This gives a clean cut, for the clay does not stick to it as it would to a spade.

When a potter makes a large rough jar, he coils a rolled strip of clay in layers as he walks around a stand. After each round, he hammers the strip down with a wooden mallet, continuing until the sides are as high as he wishes. The damp jar is then pounded inside and out, the mallet dipped frequently in water to keep the clay from sticking, erasing the lines of the coils. The round prints made by the blows of the mallet are unintentionally decorative.

Smaller and finer pieces are made on a potter's wheel, an invention of the ancient Chinese. The Thai wheel is mounted on a metal pin at the top of a low post set in the ground. Two workers sit on the ground. One turns the wheel, while the other dexterously works on a lump of clay, shaping it with his wet, slippery hands.

If it is a simple jar, it is soon removed from the wheel. A girl shapes it further with a wooden paddle, and flattens the bottom so that it will stand. When there are knobs, handles, or solid decorations, they are molded separately and added. Then the object is set aside to dry.

When the work is dry a pattern can be painted on with slip. This is clay ground very fine and mixed with water to a creamy consistency. It may be used in its natural color, a different clay from that used in the pottery, or color may be added. The objects are again dried; then they are ready to be fired in the kiln.

The kiln is a large brick oven. It has a low antechamber, like an igloo, which holds the wood for burning. The pottery is stacked in the main chamber with great care, each on a clay disk and sprinkled with straw ashes to keep the pieces from firing together. The opening is bricked up and the fire started. Broken, discarded pots are piled above and around the kiln to help with the insulation.

After two days the kiln is allowed to cool gradually, and then the contents are removed. If glaze is desired, the pottery is now ready for it. The glaze is made of silica mixed with lime, potash, and tin, which forms a hard, shining finish. Decorations can be painted on before the glaze is added, or they may be painted on over the fired glaze, then refired in a smaller kiln with less heat.

There are several ways to apply the glaze: it may be brushed on with even strokes, blown on through a bamboo tube, or the object may be dipped in a bath of glaze.

As in Sukhodaya, architectural ornaments and roofing tiles are still made in Thailand. They are covered with colored glazes: orange, blue, green, or yellow. The tiles are flat with rounded edges and overlap on the roof like the scales of a dragon. Small, gleaming tiles are made to cover the carved ends of the eaves.

Ceramics have been used in the temples and palaces for generations. Small bits of porcelain decorate the walls of the buildings in bands of intricate designs or all-over patterns.

The Phra Prang of one temple towers over Bangkok. Two hundred and fifty feet high, it is surrounded by four smaller spires. The surface is decorated with many thousands of pieces of fine crockery — whole dishes and bowls, and many pieces broken into petal shapes. All are set right into the masonry. The broken bits look like flowers unless studied closely.

Steep, narrow steps mount nearly to the top of the Phra Prang. From this vantage point one can get a marvelous view across the city. Bangkok is cut with silver ribbons of canals. From that height they do not look like the muddy thoroughfares they are. Tiled and thatched roofs of temples, government buildings, houses, and huts form a many-colored patchwork among the trees. On the opposite side of the busy river are the spires and shining roofs of the king's palace and temple, looking as though they were entirely the works of skillful potters. Beyond the palace rise the orange tiled roofs of the National Museum where many varieties of beautiful ceramics of the past are on exhibition.

And so the city, built on mud dug from the canals, has been made beautiful by mud fashioned by craftsmen into the colorful ornaments of living.

21

Trade Yesterday and Today

"Ten kinds of wares are not worth one rich paddy field."

Bangkok's busy airport is only twenty-seven hours away from the furthest countries. It used to take eight months or more to make the journey in sailing ships from Europe. For centuries the ports of Thailand have been on the trade routes between India, China, and Japan, and goods were exchanged with bordering countries by pony, bullock, and elephant caravans.

The Portuguese, in 1511, were the first Europeans to come to Thailand. Sailing around the tip of Africa, they reached the East Indies and pressed onwards, searching for spices.

Before the invention of refrigeration, spices were almost worth their weight in gold because of their importance in the preservation of food, as well as being prized for flavorings and as an ingredient in perfumes, cosmetics, and medicines. The search for spices and the spice trade helped to open up the world. Voyages to Asia and back lasted several years, and the real and imagined dangers of unknown seas forced up spice prices. Cloves, cinnamon, and pepper were among those most prized.

In what is now Thailand, spices were part of the revenue paid to the king, and among the gifts which he sent to foreign rulers. The Thai trade in pepper has declined in importance, but some is still exported. Trade was carried on through one of the king's ministers, called the *Phra Klang*, and at one time only rice, hides, sugar, lumber, and iron were traded without passing through the hands of the king's minister. At any time new items might be added to the list. Permission might be granted for the exchange of merchandise and then revoked on short notice.

Foreigners lived in trading posts, called "factories," on the outskirts of the Thai ports. They were allowed to carry on their customs and religions without interference.

The system of royal monopoly came about naturally, for revenue from the provinces was paid in produce. It was the usual form of trade in the Orient, but often carried with it the evils of necessary bribes.

The storehouses were called "godowns" and were packed with goods from all over the country. They were aromatic with spices, gums, tree oil, tobacco, sugar, wax, lumber, and sweet-smelling dyes. These odors combined with the reek of fish and hides of deer and buffaloes. There were also stores of ivory tusks, horns, edible birds' nests, and tortoise shell. Betel leaves and areca nuts were in demand throughout the Indies for chewing.

Elephants were exported to India for her armies. The elephants were transported in ships that carried great loads of banana trees — stems and leaves intact. Each animal ate approximately seventy trees during the voyage. The ships crossed the Bay of Bengal from the port of Mergui, a dependency of Ayudhya.

Mergui was an important fortified port at the mouth of the Tenasserim River on the western side of the Malay Peninsula, in what is now Burma. Ships from India could reach Mergui in three weeks; the journey to Ayudhya took about two more. The distance around the tip of the Malay Peninsula was about three times as far, and ships were six months on the voyage from India. Winds and currents were variable. The ships tacked — and sometimes had to anchor — in order to change course, sending out a longboat to tow the ship about. The Strait of Malacca was infested with pirates. True, some pirates lurked among the maze of forested, rocky islands near Mergui, but they were not as numerous.

From Mergui, ships and barges loaded with merchandise could go up the tidal river, through hot, steamy mangrove swamps to the town of Tenasserim. Here the goods were transferred to smaller boats. The larger ones could not navigate the river further for it became narrow and swift. It ran through impenetrable forests full of animals — elephants, prowling tigers, and rhinoceroses (which were believed to be carnivorous). Travelers slept in their

boats, prey to ravenous mosquitoes. These forests are still wild and unexplored today.

When the river became shallow, the goods were carried by land in bullock carts or by porters over a rough track that led across a pass through the jungle-clad mountains. The track became a road on the east coast that ran through cultivated land to a port, where the goods were loaded on ships to be taken to Ayudhya. Ships were held up at the mouth of the river, cargoes examined, and a tax paid. The king had an option on all merchandise before it could be traded in the open market.

After the fall of Ayudhya, trade moved to Bangkok. The river was crowded with brigs and schooners from the West and junks from China. The junks made one voyage a year from China and stayed in port for two months, selling their cargoes and loading for the return trip. The junks lined up, joined together by gangplanks. Under awnings stretched over the decks to keep off rain and the heat of the sun, merchandise was spread out on display. The loud banging of gongs announced across the water that all was ready. The junk soon became a noisy, floating bazaar, thronged with traders and onlookers who had come to admire the goods from foreign lands. Nearly every officer and member of the crew had invested in some part of the cargo and each sat beside his wares, ready to shout out their virtues. They were all closely watched by Thai officials to see that no opium was smuggled into the city.

Trade was carried on in much the same way until the middle of the nineteenth century, when King Mongkut signed agreements between Thailand and foreign nations. Trade became free to all. Aliens could now own land and travel around the country without restrictions. Duties

There is always heavy traffic on the Thai rivers. Here
boat vendors peddle their wares to water-front shops.

were fixed instead of fluctuating, although the government
still kept a few monopolies.

Since that time commerce has grown enormously. In
Thailand's natural products and manufactured goods, her
exports in rice, tin, rubber, and lumber lead.

Manufacturing plants turn out textiles, fibers, leather,
cement, bricks, pottery, and many other things. Most of
the export trade goes through the port of Bangkok. The
bar at the mouth of the river has been dredged, and now
large ships can enter the river and anchor at piers.

Sawmills, rice mills, and sugar refineries line the banks

of the river at Bangkok. Owing to zoning laws, however, most of the larger factories, where goods for home and foreign trade are made, are in the outskirts, or on the canals that stretch from the city.

Articles from Thailand and from all over the world are sold in cosmopolitan Bangkok. The streets are lined with shops run by Chinese, Indians, and Thai selling useful, everyday articles and foods. There are shops that cater to the ever-increasing tourist trade with glass cases displaying their wares; some of these are beautiful and others somewhat tawdry.

There are crowded market places, and the old water marts still exist where boats, carrying various wares, jam together.

Largely because of trade and commerce, and the enlightened policy of her kings from the middle of the nineteenth century, Thailand has acquired much from European culture in the last couple hundred years. Yet she has managed, at the same time, to keep her own individuality and the best traditions and charm of her past. Thailand today is a prosperous and modern nation.

Bibliography

Bacon, George B.: *Siam, the Land of the White Elephant*. New York: Charles Scribner; 1873.

Bhirasri, Professor Silpa: *The Origin and Evolution of Thai Murals*. Bangkok: Fine Arts Department; 1959.

Blanchard, Wendell: "Thailand." *Human Relations Area Files*. New Haven: Hraf Press; 1957.

Bowie, Theodore, Ed.: *The Arts of Thailand*. Bloomington: Indiana University Press; 1960.

Cartwright, B. O., translator: *Turpin's History of Siam*. Bangkok: American Presbyterian Mission Press; 1908.

Chakrabongse, H.R.H. Prince Chula: *Lords of Life*. London: Alvin Redman, Ltd.; 1960.

De Choisy, L'Abbe. *Journal au Suite du Voyage de Siam*. Amersterdam: P. Mortier; 1687.

de Young: *Village Life In Modern Thailand*. Berkeley: University of California Press; 1955.

Collins, Maurice: *Siamese White*. London: Faber and Faber Ltd.; 1951.

Commaille, J.: *Guide Aux Ruines D'Angkor*. Paris: Librairie Hatchette et Cie; 1912.

Elvin, Harold: *Avenue to the Door of the Dead*. London: Anthony Bond Ltd.; 1961.

Feroci, Professor C.: *Siamese Painting*. Bangkok; 1928.

Graham, Walter A.: *Siam*. London: Alexander Moring; 1924.

Government Fine Arts Department: *The Classical Dances*. Bangkok: 1961.

Government of Thailand Board of Investments: *Opportunities for Industry in Thailand*. Bangkok: Ramin Press; 1960.

Government Publicity Bureau: *Siam*. Bangkok: World's Fair Edition.

Government Tourist Bureau: *Democratic Thailand*. Bangkok: Public Relations Department; 1957.

Journal of the Siam Society. Vol. 1 to 28. Bangkok; 1904 to 1935.

Kaufman, Howard K.: *Bangkhaud, A Community Study in Thailand*. New York: Association for Asian Studies; 1960.

Landon, Kenneth Perry: *Siam in Transition*. Chicago: University of Chicago Press; 1939.

Bibliography

Le May, Reginald: *An Asian Arcady.* Cambridge, England: Hefler; 1926.
Leonowens, Anna: *English Governess at the Siamese Court.* Boston: Fields Orgood & Co.; 1870.
Moffat, Abbot Low: *Mongkut, the King of Siam.* Ithaca: Cornell University Press; 1961.
Mouhot, Henri: *Travels in the Central Parts of Indochina (Siam).* London: J. Murray; 1864.
Neal, Fred Arthur: *Narrative of a Residence in the Kingdom of Siam.* London: Bradbury and Evans; 1852.
Office of Commercial Counsellor, Compiler: *Thailand.* Bangkok; 1957.
Pallegoix, Mgr.: *Description du Royaume Thai du Siam.* Paris: Lagny; 1854.
Phronthuchitr, P.: *Buddhist Art and Architecture.* Bangkok
Sarasas, Phra: *My Country, Thailand.* Bangkok: Chatra Press; 1956.
Seidenfaden, E.: *Guide to Bangkok.* Bangkok: Royal State Railways; 1932.
Smith, Malcolm: *A Physician at the Court of Siam.* London: Country Life Ltd.; 1947.
Thai Digest Reprint on Sericulture. Bangkok: Surisak Press.
Thai Culture Series. The Fine Arts Department: Bangkok, Thailand.
Bhirasri, Prof. Silpa: *Thai Buddhist Art and Architecture.* 1959.
——: *An Appreciation of Sukhothai Art.* 1962.
——: *Contemporary Art in Thailand.* 1960.
——: *Thai Lacquer Works.* circa 1960
——: *Thai Wood Carvings.* 1961.
Bridhyakorn, H.H. Prince Dhaninvat Kromamun Bidyalabh: *The Nang.*
—— & Yupho, Dhanit: *The Khon.* 1962.
Duriyanga, Phra Chen: *Thai Music.* 1962.
Griswold, A. B.: *What is a Buddha Image?* 1962.
—— & Buribhand, Luang Boribal: *Thai Images of the Buddha.* 1962.
Rajadhon, Phya Anuman: *Introducing Cultural Thailand.* 1962
——: *Thai Literature In Relation to the Diffusion of her Culture.* 1961.
——: *The Thai Language.* 1960.
Yupho, Dhanit: *Khon Masks.* 1962.
Thompson, Virginia: *Thailand, the New Siam.* New York: Macmillan; 1941.
Vella, Walter F.: *Siam Under Rama III.* Locust Valley, New York: Published for the Association of Asian Studies by J. J. Augustin, Inc.; 1957.
Wales, H. G. Quaritch: *Siamese State Ceremonies.* London: Bernard Quaritch Ltd.; 1931.
Wells, Kenneth Elmer: *Buddhism in Thailand.* Edinburgh: International Review of Missions; 1942.
——: *Thai Buddhism, Its Rites and Activities.* Bangkok: Bangkok Times Press; 1939.

Index

Index

About the Author

Margaret Ayer lived in Thailand for many years when her father was Advisor in Public Health for the government, and she had friends who were members of the royal family. She studied art in Rome, Paris, and Philadelphia, and has had several exhibitions of her work in the Far East. Three of her paintings, which were exhibited in Bangkok, were purchased by His Majesty King Prajahipok of Thailand.

A recent trip to Thailand reaffirmed Margaret Ayer's love for the country. It was on this latest trip that she collected much of her material for MADE IN THAILAND.

Margaret Ayer and her husband, Alfred Babington Smith, make their winter home in New York's Greenwich Village and summer in Easton, Connecticut. She is the author-illustrator of eight books for children and, as a free-lance artist, has illustrated over 150 more.

A Note on the Type

The text of this book is set in Caledonia, a Lino-
type face designed by W. A. Dwiggins (1880-
1956), who was responsible for so much that is
good in contemporary book design. Though much
of his early work was in advertising, Mr. Dwiggins later devoted his prolific talents to book and
type design and worked with great distinction in
both fields. In addition to his designs for Caledonia, he created the Metro, Electro, and Eldo-
rado series of type faces, as well as a number of
exceptional cuttings that have never been issued
commercially.

Caledonia belongs to the family of printing
types printers called "modern face" — a term used
to mark the change in style of type-letters that
occurred at the end of the eighteenth century. It
is best evidenced in the letter shapes designed by
Baskerville, Martin, Bodoni, and the Didots.

Typography by Atha Tehon.

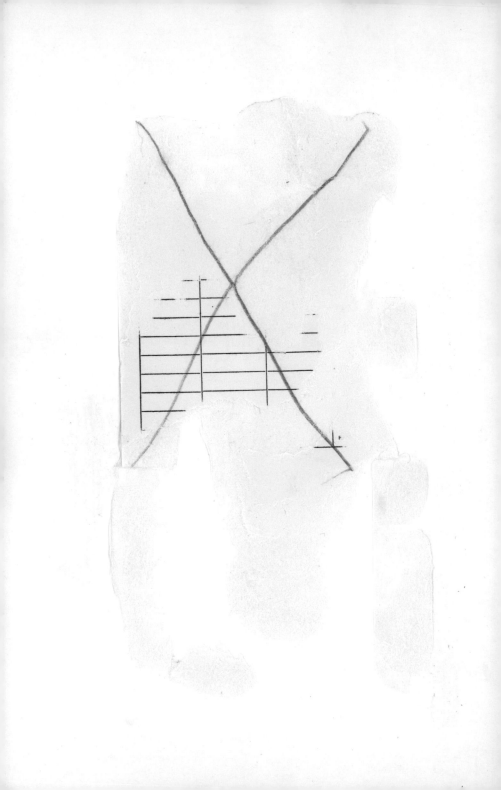